ARS THEURGIA GOETIA

FOUNDATIONS OF PRACTICAL SORCERY VOLUME IV

FOUNDATIONS OF PRACTICAL SORCERY VOLUME IV

ARS THEURGIA GOETIA

BEING AN ACCOUNT AND RENDITION OF THE ARTE AND PRAXIS OF THE
CONJURATION OF SOME OF THE SPIRITS OF SOLOMON

Gary St. M. Nottingham

Published by Avalonia
www.avaloniabooks.co.uk

Published by Avalonia

BM Avalonia
London
WC1N 3XX
England, UK
www.avaloniabooks.co.uk

ISBN 978-1-905297-77-1

Design by Satori, for Avalonia.

British Library Cataloguing in Publication Data. A catalogue record for this book is available from the British Library.

About the Author

Gary St. M. Nottingham's commitment to the study and practice of the alchemical arte, ritual magic, grimoires and spirit conjuration means that he can often be found peering at bubbling flasks or a shewstone – or otherwise engaged in deepening his knowledge and understanding of such matters. His practices also draw on the work of the 17th-century astrologer William Lilly and the arte of horary astrology.

Gary was raised in south Shropshire, where, during his mid-teens, he became involved with a small Coven, thereby gaining an excellent grounding in a wide selection of magical practices. Following the conjuration of a spirit, and asking it for help that manifested when least expected, he subsequently became involved with a group of practising alchemists. He has a background in horticulture, enjoys spending time in the garden and playing chess. He organised the legendary Ludlow Esoteric Conference (2004-2008), helped produce *Verdelet* occult magazine, has taught many free day workshops on basic occult skills and is a popular speaker at esoteric conferences.

The seven volumes of *Foundations of Practical Sorcery* are an unabridged collection of Gary's much sought-after previously published work, updated and made available to a wider readership at last.

Table of Contents

IINTRODUCTION 8

OF THAT MOST SECRET ARTE.. 11

OF THE FOUR EMPERORS 14

OF THOSE SPIRITS DARKSOME AND DIVINE 28

THE WANDERING PRINCES..117

PRAXIS...151

INDEX 168

Introduction

Foundations of Practical Sorcery

We live in an age where we are awash with information on all subjects, and to this the magical artes are no exception. Whilst the student of magic can easily access all manner of electronic files there is nothing quite like a book.

A book can not only be picked up and read, but will, in many instances, over time, become a friend, guide and teacher who has assisted the reader on their journey throughout their life. Quite simply books can change lives and this is why those who have been in positions of power through the centuries have tried, and often failed, to keep knowledge out of the hands of everyday folk. This is perhaps primarily because they feared the power of the book to cause change, and change is what the seven books in the Foundations of Practical Sorcery series will cause.

Today the magical artes have never been so accessible, although that doesn't mean the demands that the arte makes upon the practitioner have been lessened in any way. While the arte is, in principle, for all, not everyone will have the self-discipline, the will and the imagination to succeed therein. However for those who do have these basic attributes or are prepared to acquire them there is much to be gained from the practice of magic in all levels of life. For many people their ingress into the arte will be by books, and the exploration of and working with the information they contain. There is nothing like experience even if your magic proves less successful than hoped for: there is no such thing as failure in magic, because every experience will, at the very least, teach the practitioner something, even if it's just to try harder next time!

Of course some will have access to a magical group and the knowledge and collective experience to be found therein; but for many this will not be the case. Magical groups regardless of hue by and large have much to commend them, but not all of them do. I have in the past been approached by people who have gone through a coven system yet then been led to ask me to help them practice and study magic. It seemed their coven did not in fact practice the arte; which left me wondering what was it that they did do. I am aware of similar approaches made to other magical practitioners, which has left me concluding that some magical groups and covens can actually be detrimental to an individual's magical development and understanding - although this is certainly not the case with all by any means.

Foundations of Practical Sorcery goes some way to rectifying this deficit in any student's magical life. They offer clear magical instruction and accounts of magical acts to be performed, thus making the arte easily accessible. The methods and techniques presented are all based upon my own personal knowledge and experience which goes back over forty years, methods and techniques that have worked successfully for me and will do so for any reader who applies them accordingly.

In many ways I was fortunate, during the autumn of 1972, to meet a magical practitioner who taught me much regarding the arte, generously affording me the run of their magical library as well. Having been schooled extensively in magical knowledge from my mid teen years I consider myself to have been extremely fortunate and lucky to have had many experiences not easily available to many people. Thus the present Foundations of Practical Sorcery series is the distillation of four decades of successful magical workings.

Each of the seven volumes gives a clear account and rendition of one or another area of magical instruction that I have received and have been taught. They are presented to the reader in a clear and workable style which will provide them with a concise and firm foundation, allowing the serious magical student to explore the Western Magical Tradition, the inheritance of us all.

Gary St. M. Nottingham, February 2015

Gary St. M. Nottingham

CHAPTER ONE

Of that most secret Arte

This work is an interpretation of the seals of the second part of the Solomonic grimoire cycle, *Theurgia-Goetia*. Surprisingly *Theurgia Goetia* is little known; but it does offer useful ingress into the arte of angelic conjuration. This is a work that is concerned with a mixture of spirits, whom are considered to be both good and bad, and it is clearly influenced by the *Steganographia* of the late fifteenth century abbot Trithemius; who was highly influential on the magical careers of both Agrippa and Paracelsus.

Whether either of these two highly influential sixteenth century occultists was responsible for this work is not known; but they were certainly the right people in the right place at the right time. In some respects this is a work that is a ritualised version of the *Steganographia*, and what is different in its approach to other works of the various grimoire cycles is its insistence on the cardinal points to evoke the angelic spirits.

As can be seen by the texts each spirit has a direction from which it is evoked into the shewstone of the arte that is placed upon the altar. Yet unlike other grimoires the spirits involved all seem to have much the same office to perform. The spirits are considered to be of an airy nature and who wander at will throughout creation. Because of their airy nature they are deemed to be more easily accessible if their evocation takes place in an upstairs room, as opposed to being conjured at ground level. Whether this is something to take note of I will leave to others to decide for themselves.

Much of the praxis is drawn from the *Goetia*; the magical circle, which is detailed therein, is suggested to be suitable for the work. Although I would suggest other designs, that which is from the Solomonic cycle will suffice, as would those that are based on the four names of God and the archangels of the elements, as this is a work that is related to the four compass points, by a plenitude of ministering spirits whose offices are curiously all one. That is they are firstly of both a good and evil nature, and they are subservient to their princes who each have an abode at a compass point.

Therefore when they are conjured they must be approached from their relevant elemental quarter; that is the conjuror will need to face the relevant compass point for their summoning. As with the *Goetia*, the seal of the spirit must be worn on the breast as a lamen, as well as a seal being placed under the shewstone of the arte. The office of these spirits are all one and the same, they can show all that the conjuror should ask, regardless of where it is, or what it is that the operator wishes to know.

Whilst they can also show any secret that a person has and can make it come to light, they can also achieve anything that is the will of the conjuror. The conjurations are the same for each of the spirits; simply change the spirit's name as required. It will be noted that additional conjurations as laid down in the *Steganographia* are also included for the use in the conjuration of the spirit.

The Compass Rose

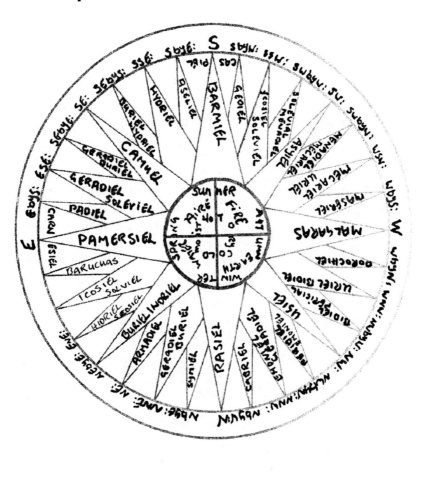

CHAPTER TWO

Of the Four Emperors

Firstly there are four Emperors whose dwellings are at the compass points. Of these, the first is in the east, and is the chief spirit, is considered to be great and to rule in the east. He has under his dominion one thousand great dukes and also one hundred lesser dukes. He also has 6,000,000,000,000 ministering spirits. There are also twelve dukes who are considered to be of good service.

Seal of Carnesiel to be drawn in red inks:

The traditional conjuration for this spirit from the *Steganographia* is given thus and can be used with the traditional evocationary formula.

> '*Carnesiel aphoys chemeryn mear aposyn. Layr pean noema ovear ma sere cratly Caleco thorteam chameron ianoar pelyn layr baduson iesy melros ionatiel delassar rodivial meron savean fabelron clumarsy preos throen benarys favean demosynon laernoty Camdenton.*

Of the seals of the twelve dukes of Carnesiel to be drawn in red inks:

Myresyn:

Benoham:

Armany:

Ornich:

Aresiel:

Capriel:

Zabriel:

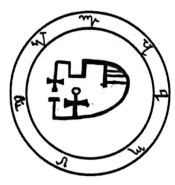

Laphor:

Vadriel:

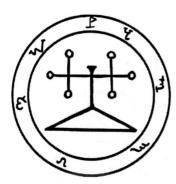

Bedary:

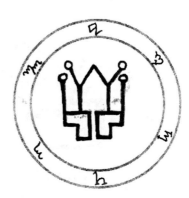

Capriel:

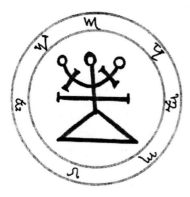

Cumeriel:

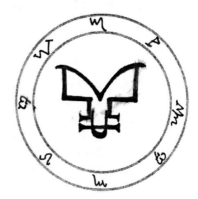

Caspiel

Caspiel is the great and chief emperor who rules in the south. He has at his command two hundred great dukes and he also has four hundred lesser dukes under him and 1,000,200,000,000 ministering spirits. These spirits are much inferior. Of the many spirits, twelve dukes are given to be of use, the *Steganographia* says that they will obey you and that they are of good disposition. However the lesser spirits who attend upon them are churlish and stubborn by nature; but they will, according to Trithemius, become more obedient if the conjuror is firm and unperturbed. Their seals are to be drawn in red inks.

This is his traditional conjuration:

'Caspiel asbyr Chameronty churto freveon dayr fabelron Cathurmy
meresyn elso peanotailtran Caspio fuar Medon clibarsy caberosyn ulty pean vearches pemasy natolbyr meldary cardenopen men for diviel adro.'

The seals of the twelve dukes under Caspiel:

Ursiel:

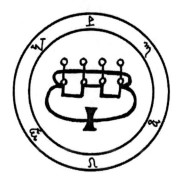

Budarim:

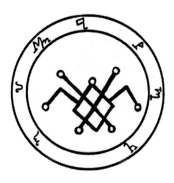

Geriel:

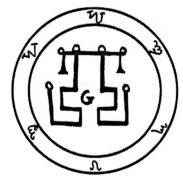

Ambri:

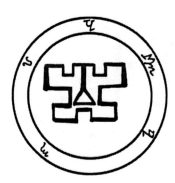

Chariel:

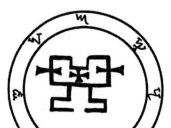

Maras:

Aridiel:

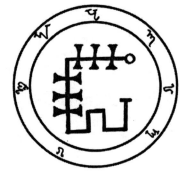

Oriel:

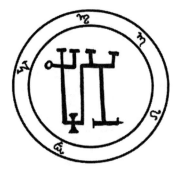

Femol:

Larmol:

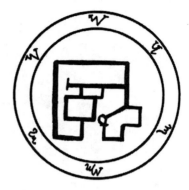

Camor:

Camory:

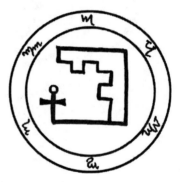

Amenadiel

Amenadiel is the spirit who is supreme in the west and has three hundred greater dukes and five hundred lesser dukes under his command, and innumerable spirits. He may be called at any hour of the day. Of these spirits twelve are given, however they are to be called in their appropriate hour. Each spirit is associated with a two-hour period starting at the first hour of the day with Vadros, then the second two-hour period will be given to Camiel, following this formula the last spirit to be associated with the last two-hour period of the day will be Nadroc. The seal of Amenadiel and his spirits is to be drawn in blue inks.

This is his traditional conjuration

> *'Amenadiel aprolsy chameronta nosroy throen mesro salayr chemaros noe pean larsy freveon ionatiel pelroyn rathroy Caser malusan pedon Cranochyran daboy seor marchosy lavo pedar venoti Gesroy phernotiel Cabron.'*

The seals of the twelve dukes of Amenadiel:

Vadros:

Camiel:

Luziel:

Musiriel:

Rapsiel:

Lamael:

Zoeniel:

Curifas:

Almesiel:

Codriel:

Balsur:

Nadroc:

Demoriel

Demoriel is a great and mighty emperor of the north. He has four hundred greater dukes and six hundred lesser dukes that are under his command. The dukes have 700,000,800,000,900,000 spirits at their command whereof we will declare but twelve and their seals. The seals are to be drawn in black inks. Each of the spirits are associated with a two-hour period starting at sunrise in the order of spirits that are given. The conjuration must be given facing the northern quarter wherein they dwell.

This is his traditional conjuration:

'Demoriel onear dabursoy Cohyne chamerson ymeor pean olayr chelrusys noeles schemlaryn venodru patron myselro chadarbon vevaon maferos ratigiel personay lodiol camedon nasiel fabelmerusin sosiel chamarchoysyn.'

The seals of the twelve dukes of Demoriel:

Arnibiel:

Cabarim:

Menador:

Burisiel:

Doriel:

Mador:

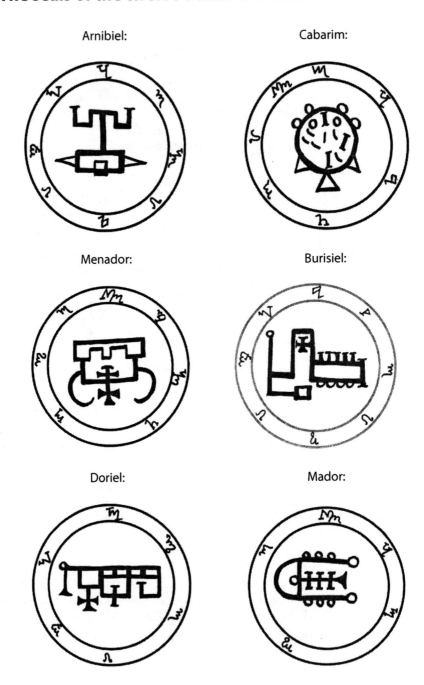

Carnol:

Dubilon:

Medar:

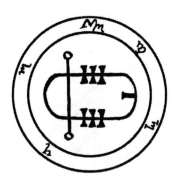

Churibal:

Dabrinos:

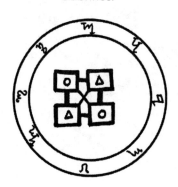

Chamiel:

CHAPTER THREE

Of those Spirits Darksome and Divine

Pamersiel

Pamersiel is the first and the chief spirit in the east under Carnesiel. He has one thousand spirits under his command; they may be summoned only during the day and with great care as they are lofty and stubborn. They obey no one unless bound by oaths for they do not obey novices in this arte. Their seals are to be drawn in yellow inks.

His traditional conjuration:

> 'Pamersiel oshurmy delmuson Thafloin peano charustea melany, lyaminto colchan,payroys, madyn, moerlay, bulre + atloor don melcove peloin ibutsyl meon mysbreath alini driaco person. Crisolnay, lemon asosle mydar, icoriel pean. Thalmon, asophiel il notreon banyel ocrimos estevor naelma befrona thulaomor fronian beldodrayn bon otalmesgo mero fas elnathyn boframoth.'

Anoyr: Madriel:

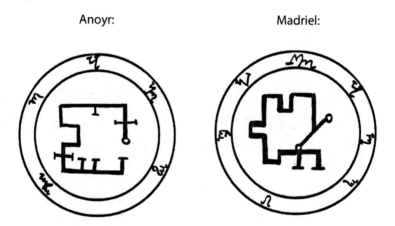

Ebra:

Sotheano:

Abrulges:

Ormenu:

Itules:

Rablion:

Hamorphiel:

Itrasbiel:

Nadrel:

Padiel

Padiel is the second spirit under the Emperor of the East and he rules in the south-east. He governs ten thousand spirits by day and twenty thousand by night. These spirits are all good by nature but they have no power of themselves other than that which is granted by their king. Therefore no seals are given for them.

His traditional conjuration:

> 'Padiel aporsy mesarpon omevas peludyn malpreaxo. Condusen ulearo thersephi bayl merphon,paroys gebuly mailthomyon ilthear tamarson acrimy lon peatha Casmy Chertiel, medony reabdo, lasonti iaciel mal atri bulomeon abry pathulmon theoma pathormyn.'

Camuel

Camuel rules also in the south-east, and has many spirits at his command; whereof we mention but ten that belong to the day and ten that are of the night. These spirits are of a comely nature and are very courteous of temperament. Their seals are to be drawn in yellow inks.

His traditional conjuration:

> 'Camuel aperoys melym mevomanial casmoyn cralty bufaco aeli lumar photirion theor besamys aneal Cabelonyr thiamo vesonthy.'

Ten spirits belonging to the day and appearing at night:

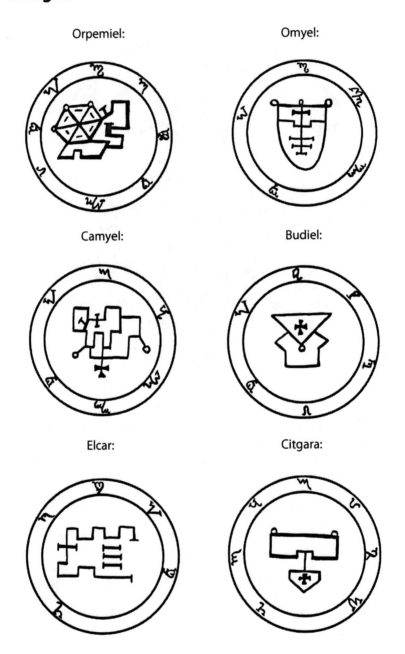

Orpemiel:

Omyel:

Camyel:

Budiel:

Elcar:

Citgara:

Pariel:

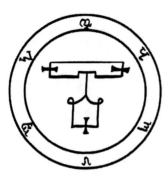

Cariel:

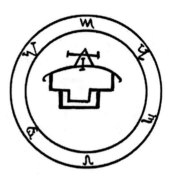

Neriel:

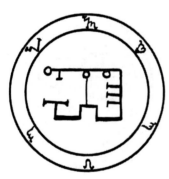

Daniel:

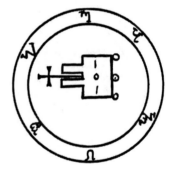

Ten spirits of the night appearing in the day:

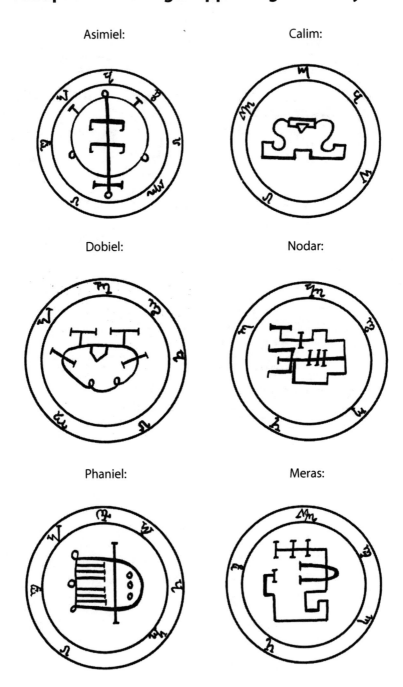

Asimiel:

Calim:

Dobiel:

Nodar:

Phaniel:

Meras:

Azemo:

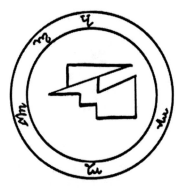

Tediel:

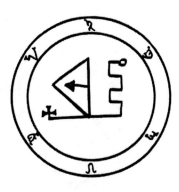

Moriel:

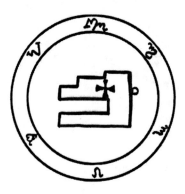

Tugaros:

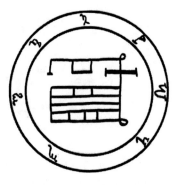

Aseliel

Aseliel is a king who is appointed to the south by eastern part of the compass. He has ten spirits that are of the day and twenty spirits that are of the night. Each of these spirits has twenty spirits who attend unto their will. These spirits are loving by nature, courteous and beautiful to behold. There seals are to be drawn in yellow inks.

His traditional conjuration:

> 'Aseliel aproysy melym, thulnear casmoyn mavear burso charny demorphaon, Theoma asmeryn diviel casponti vearly basamys ernoti chava lorson.'

The spirits of the day:

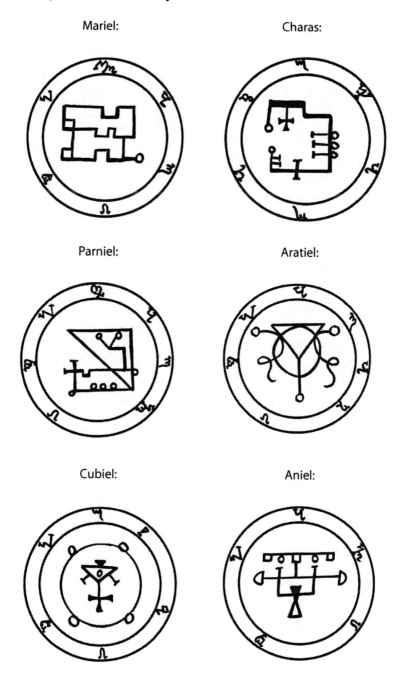

Mariel:

Charas:

Parniel:

Aratiel:

Cubiel:

Aniel:

Asahel:

Arean:

The spirits of the night:

Asphiel:

Curiel:

Chamos:

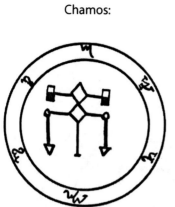

Odiel:

Melas:

Sariel:

Othiel:

Bofar:

Barmiel

Barmiel is the first and most important spirit who is under the domain of the Emperor of the South, Caspiel. He has ten dukes for the day and twenty for the night who attend unto his will. They are of a good nature and are ready to obey the conjuror; however their servants are of an arrogant nature. The seals of these spirits are to be drawn in red inks.

His traditional conjuration:

'Barmiel buras melo charnotiel malapos veno masphian albryon, chasmia pelvo morophon apluer charmya noty Mesron alraco caspiel hoalno chorbe ovear ascrea cralnoty carephon elcsor bumely nesitan army tu faron.'

The spirits of the day:

Sochas:

Tigara:

Chansi:

Keriel:

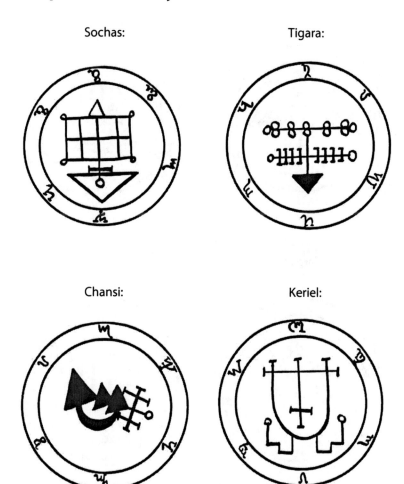

Acteras:

Barbil:

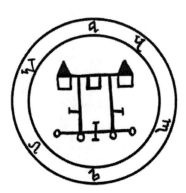

Carpiel:

Mansi:

The spirits of the night:

Barbis:

Marguns:

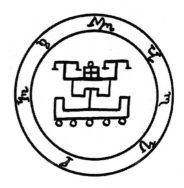

Caniel:

Acreba:

Mareaiza:

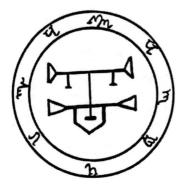

Baabal:

Gabio:

Astib:

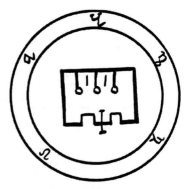

Gediel

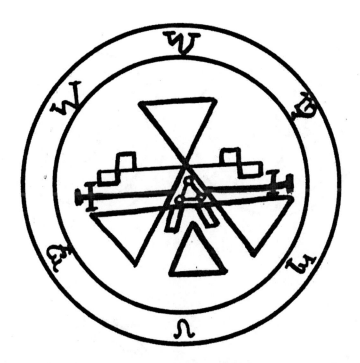

Gediel is a king who rules in the south-west and has twenty spirits who serve him in the day, and as many again in the night. These spirits are very willing to assist and they are courteous by nature and beautiful of appearance. Their seals are to be drawn in red inks. These are the seals of eight of the spirits of the day and eight of the spirits of the night.

His traditional conjuration:

'Gediel asiel modebar mopiel, casmoyn rochamurenu proys vasaron atido casmear vearsy maludym velachain demosar otiel masdurym sodiviel mesray ser amarium laveur pealo netus fabelron.'

The spirits of the day:

Coliel:

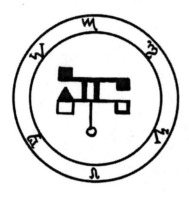

Naras:

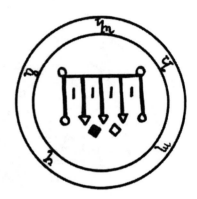

Sabas:

Assaba:

Ranciel:

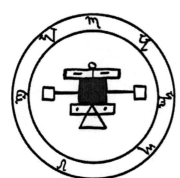

Mashel:

Sariel:

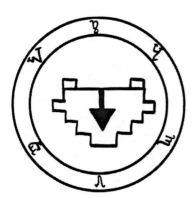

Bariel:

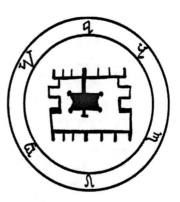

The spirits of the night:

Reciel:

Sadiel:

Agra:

Anael:

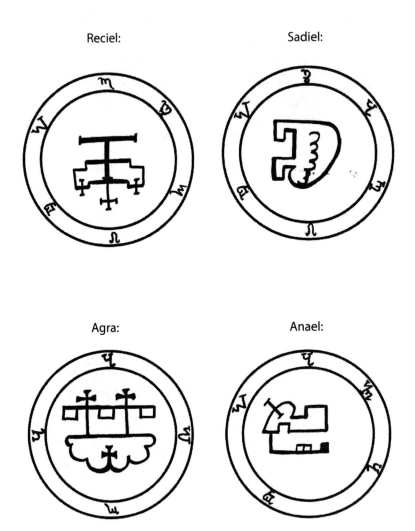

Aroan:

Cirecas:

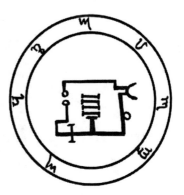

Aglas:

Vriel:

Asyriel

Asyriel is the third spirit associated with the south and he rules in the south-west of the compass. He is served by twenty dukes who attend unto him in the day and the same number who attend during the night. But of these, eight are given of the day and the same for the night. They are of a good nature and are willing to obey the conjuror. Their seals are to be drawn in red inks.

His traditional conjuration:

> *'Asyriel aphorsy Lamodyn to Carmephyn drubal asutroy sody barucon,usefer palormy thulmear asmeron chornemadusyn coleny busarethon duys marphelithubra nasaron venear fabelronty.'*

The spirits of the day:

Astor:

Carga:

Buniel:

Rabas:

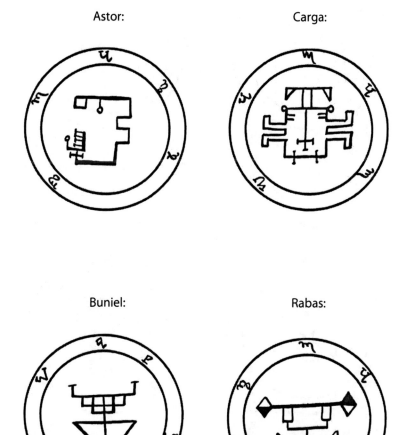

Arcisat:

Ariel:

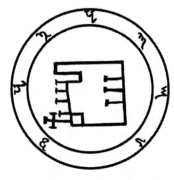

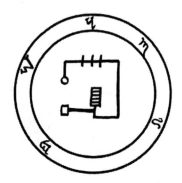

Cusiel:

Malguel:

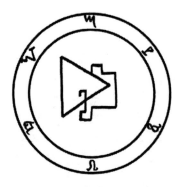

The spirits of the night:

Amiel:

Cusriel:

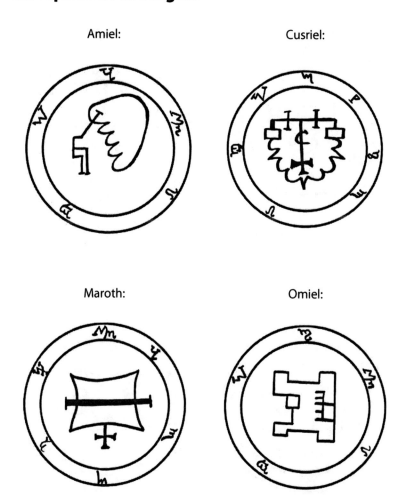

Maroth:

Omiel:

Budar:

Aspiel:

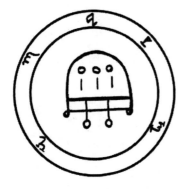

Faseau:

Hamas:

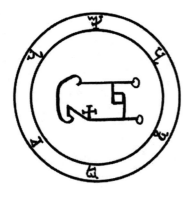

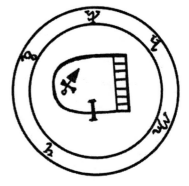

Maseriel

The fourth spirit under the Emperor of the South is Maseriel, who rules the west by south. Here given are twelve spirits of the day and twelve of the night hours. These spirits are good by nature and will perform your will in all things, for they are trust worthy. The spirits are well versed in all matters that relate unto the philosophical, magical and necromantic artes. They are peaceful by nature and appear without noise. They have themselves thirty spirits each. Their seals are to be drawn in red ink.

His traditional conjuration:

'Maseriel bulan lamodyn charnoty carmephin iabrun caresathroyn asulroy bevesy Cadumyn turiel busan Sevear almos cadufel ernoty panier iethar care pheory bulan thorty paron venio Fabelronthusy.'

The spirits of the day:

Mahue:

Roriel:

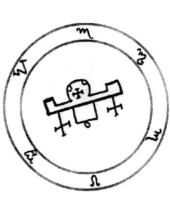

Earviel:

Zeriel:

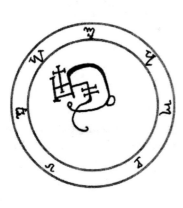

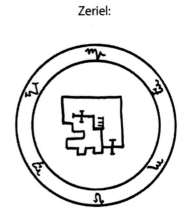

Atniel:

Vessur:

Azimel:

Chasor:

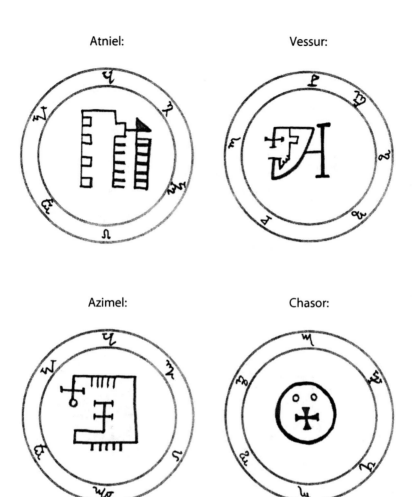

Patiel:

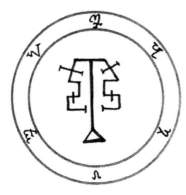

Assuel:

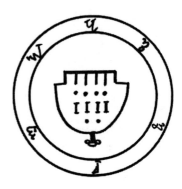

Aliel:

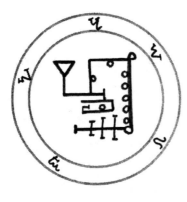

Espoel:

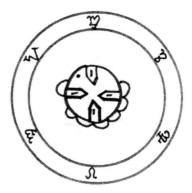

The spirits of the night:

Arach:

Maras:

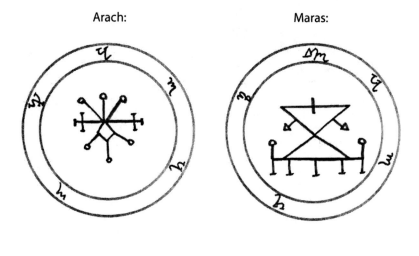

Noguiel:

Saemiel:

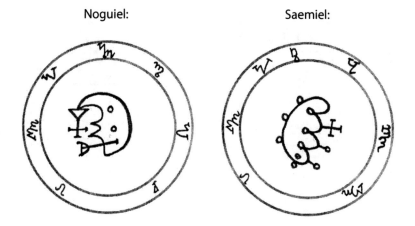

Amoyr:

Bachiel:

Baros:

Eliel:

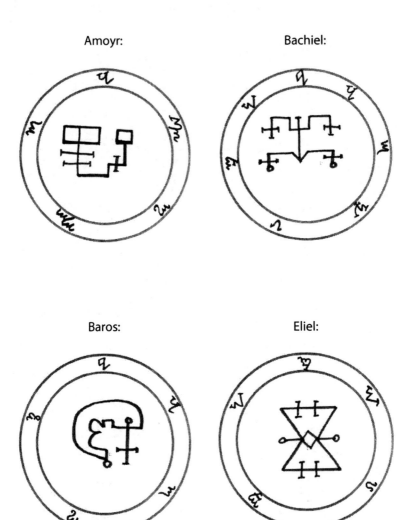

Earos:

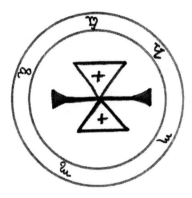

Rabiel:

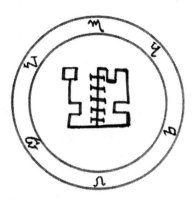

Atriel:

Salvor:

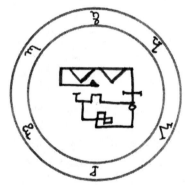

Malgaras

Malgaras is the first spirit under the Emperor of the West; he rules as a king in the west and has thirty dukes to attend unto him in the day and the same number to attend during the hours of darkness. These spirits are courteous by nature and are willing to attend to your will. They appear in pairs with their servants. The day spirits are easier to converse with than those of the night. Their seals are to be drawn in blue inks.

His traditional conjuration:

'Malgaras ador chameso bulueriny mareso bodyr Cadumir aviel casmyo redy pleoryn viordi eare viorba, chasmironty very thuriel ulnavy, bevesy mevo chasmironty naor ernyso,chony barmo calevodyn barso thubrasol.'

The spirits of the day:

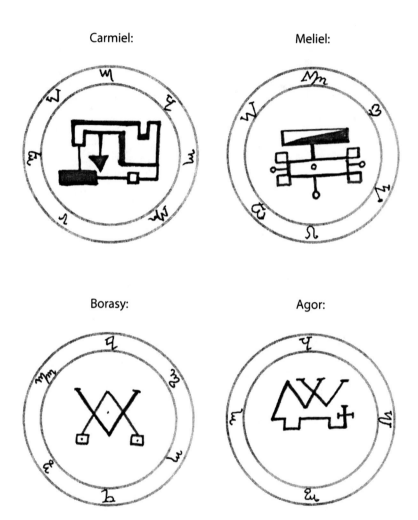

Carmiel:

Meliel:

Borasy:

Agor:

Casiel:

Rabiel:

Cabrel:

Udiel:

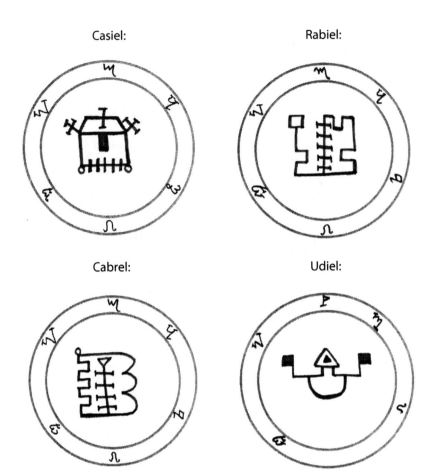

Oriel: Misiel:

Barfas: Arios:

The spirits of the night:

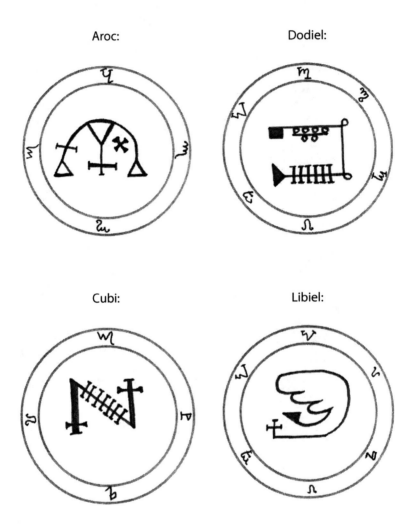

Aroc:

Dodiel:

Cubi:

Libiel:

Raboc:

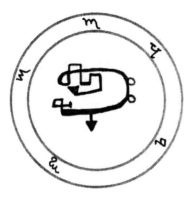

Aspiel:

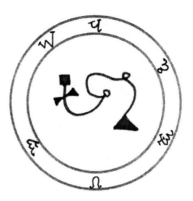

Caron:

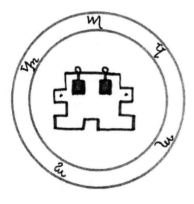

Zamor:

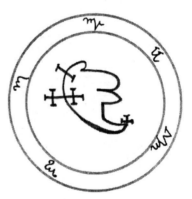

Amiel: Aspar:

Deilas: Basiel:

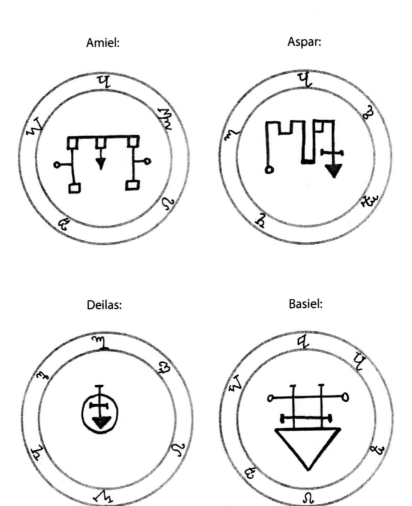

Dorochiel:

Dorochiel, sometimes known as Dorothiel, is the second spirit under the Emperor of the West. He has forty dukes who serve under him during the day time and the same at night. They are of a goodly nature and are willing to obey. This spirit is particularly useful in matters relating to the church or the gaining of positions and honours. Of the spirits, twenty-four seals are given of the day spirits and twenty-four of the night spirits. Their seals are to be drawn in blue inks.

His traditional conjuration:

'Dorochiel cusi feor madylon busar pamersy chear lanothym baony Camersy ulymeor peathan adial cadumyr renear thubra Cohagier maslon Lodierno fabelrusyn.'

The twelve dukes that are to be called before noon:

Magael:

Choriel:

Artino:

Efiel:

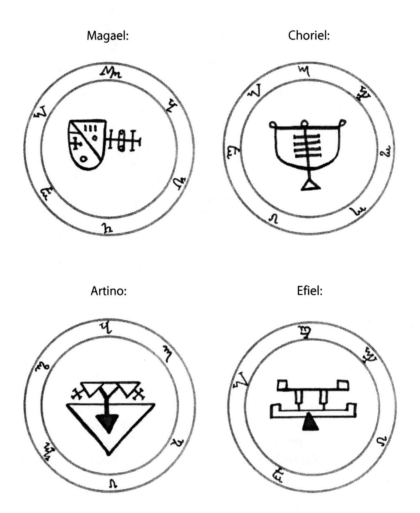

Uriel:

Arsiel:

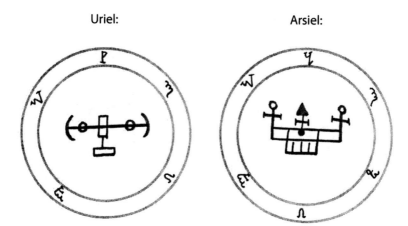

Tubiel:

Corba:

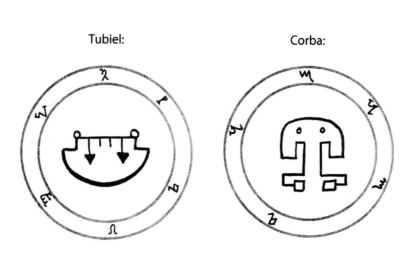

Merach:

Althor:

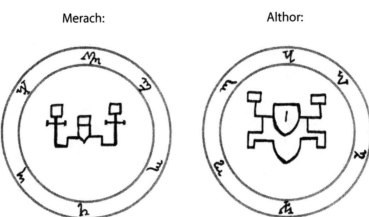

Mamel:

Omiel:

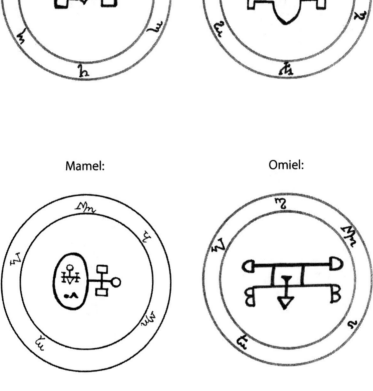

The twelve dukes to be called between noon and sunset:

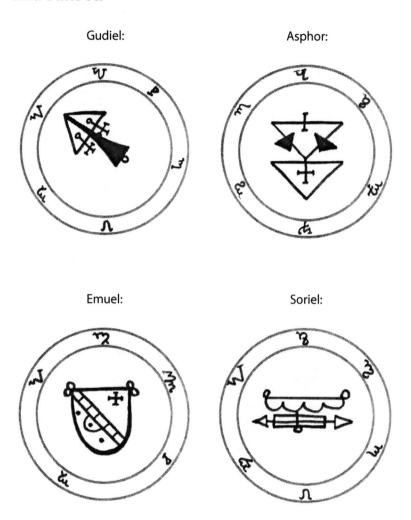

Gudiel:

Asphor:

Emuel:

Soriel:

Cabron:

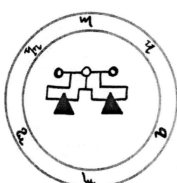

Diviel:

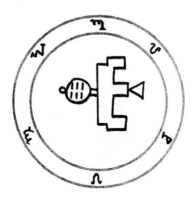

Abriel:

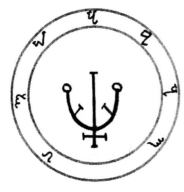

Danael:

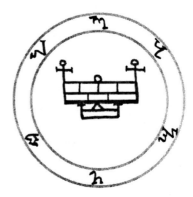

Lomor:

Casael:

Busiel:

Larfos:

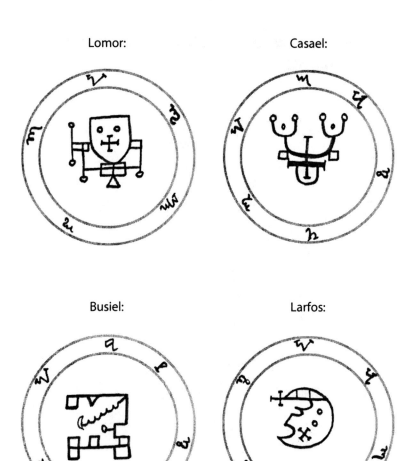

Twelve dukes who are called between sunset and midnight:

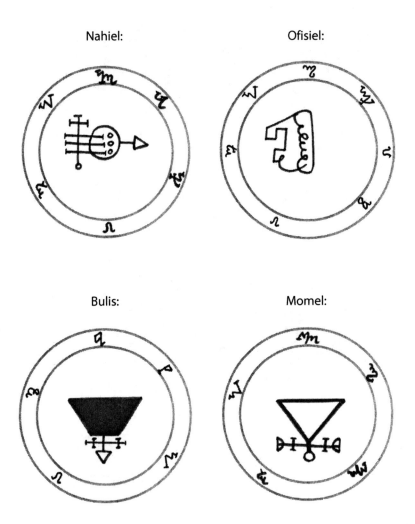

Nahiel:

Ofisiel:

Bulis:

Momel:

Darbori: Paniel:

Cursas: Aliel:

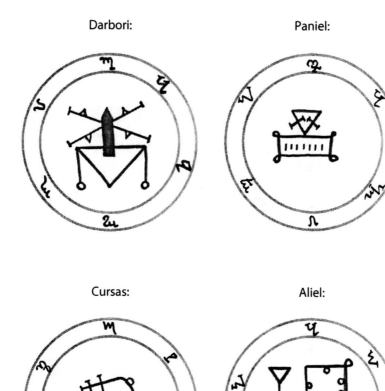

Aroziel:

Cusyne:

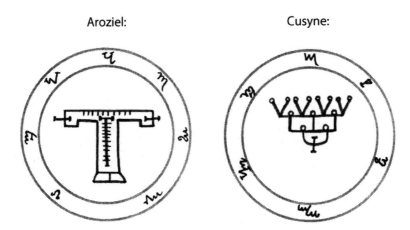

Vraniel:

Pelusar:

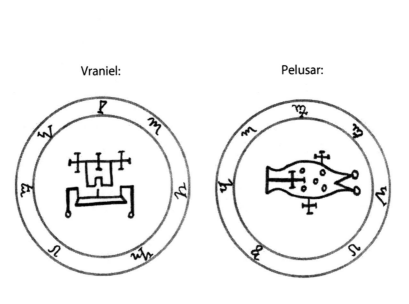

These twelve dukes are to be called between midnight and sunrise.

Pafiel:

Gariel:

Soriel:

Maziel:

Futiel: Cayros:

Narsiel: Moziel:

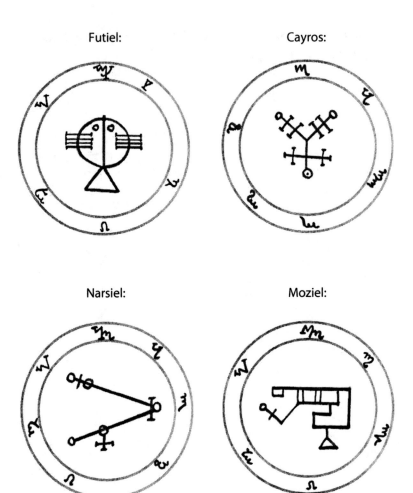

Abael:

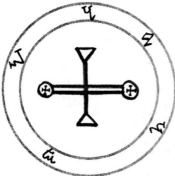

Meroth:

Cadriel:

Cadriel sigil

Lodiel:

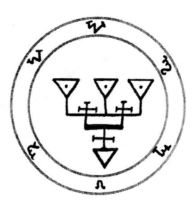

Usiel:

Usiel is a mighty prince who rules in the north-west of the compass. This spirit is served by forty spirits of the day and forty of the night time. However, of these fourteen seals of the day spirits and fourteen of the night spirits are given. These spirits are obedient to the conjuror and have power to discover treasure. They will also protect property if the seals given below are drawn on parchment and placed with that which you wish to protect. The seals are to be drawn in green inks.

His traditional conjuration:

'Usiel asoyr paremon cruato madusyn savepe mavayr realldo chameron ilco paneras thurmo pean elsoty fabel rusyn iltras charson frymasto chelmodyn.'

The fourteen dukes of the day:

Abariel:

Amenta:

Arnen:

Herne:

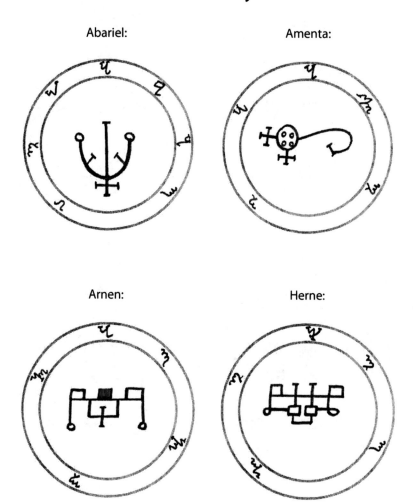

Saefer:

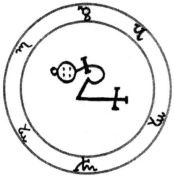

Potiel:

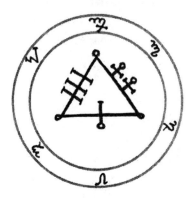

Safern:

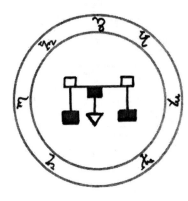

Magni:

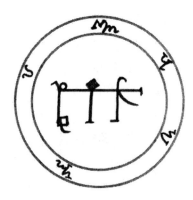

Amandiel:

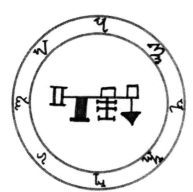

Barsu:

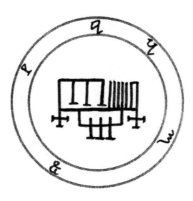

Garnasu:

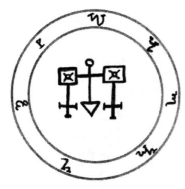

Hissam:

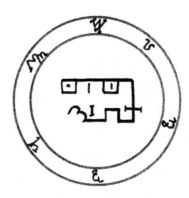

Fabariel:

Usiniel:

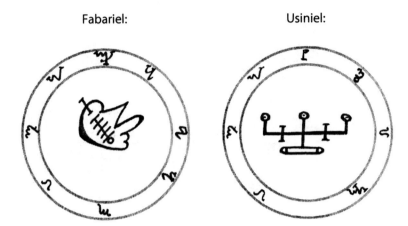

The fourteen dukes of the night:

Ansoel:

Godiel:

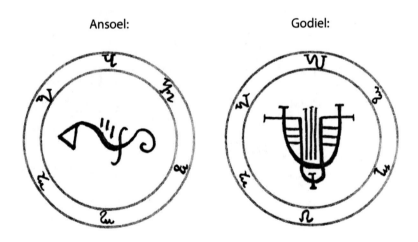

Barfos:

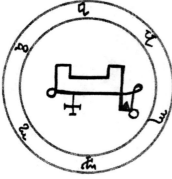

Burfa:

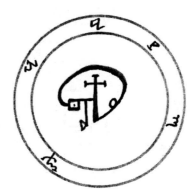

Adan:

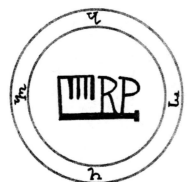

Saddiel:

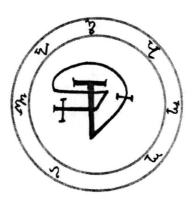

Sodiel:

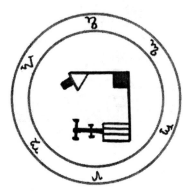

Ossiediel:

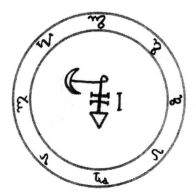

Pathier:

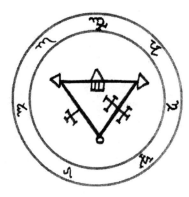

Marae:

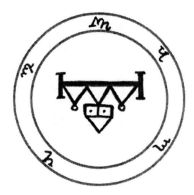

Asuriel:

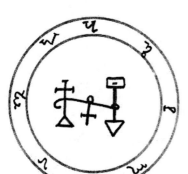

Almoel:

Las Pharon:

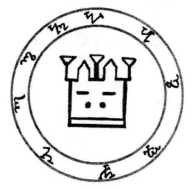

Ethiel:

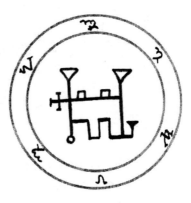

Cabariel:

Cabariel is a mighty spirit of the western quarter; he has fifty dukes that attend unto him by day and the same number by night; of whom we give the seals of ten of them that belong to the day and ten that are of the night hours. The spirits of the day are good by nature and are willing to help the conjuror; however those spirits of the night are of an evil disposition, they will deceive you if they can. Their seals are to be drawn in blue inks.

His traditional conjuration:

'Cabariel onear chameron fruant, parnaton fosiel bryosi nagteal fabelrontyn adiel thortay nofruav pean afesiel chusy.'

The seals of the ten dukes of the day:

Satifiel:

Parius:

Godiel:

Taros:

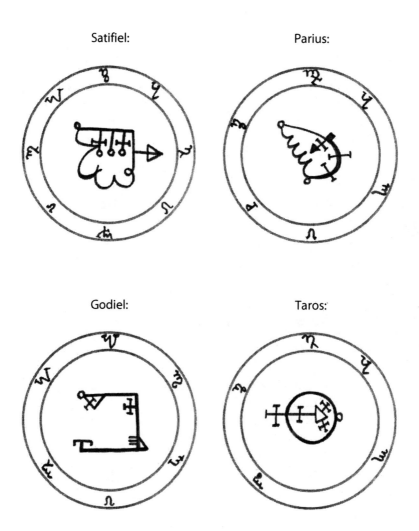

Asoriel:

Etimiel:

Clyssan:

Elitel:

Aniel:

Cuphal:

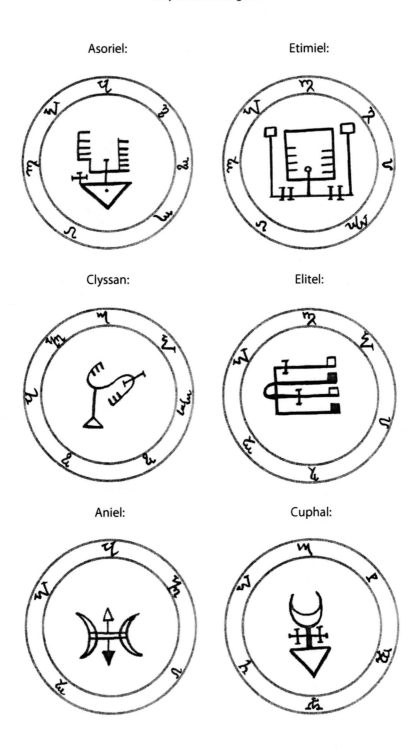

The ten dukes of the night and their seals:

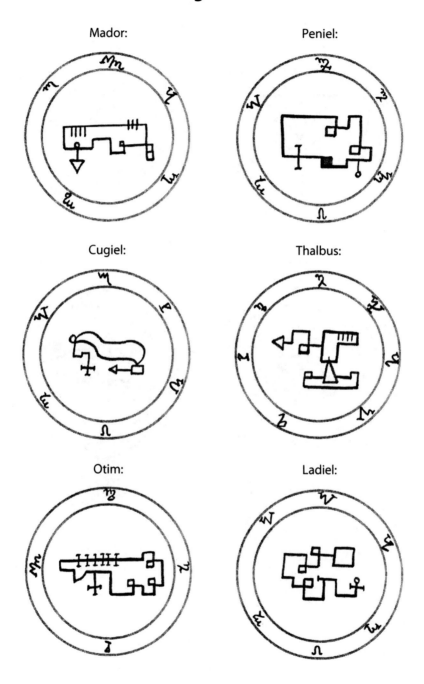

Mador:

Peniel:

Cugiel:

Thalbus:

Otim:

Ladiel:

Morias:

Pandor:

Cazul:

Dubiel:

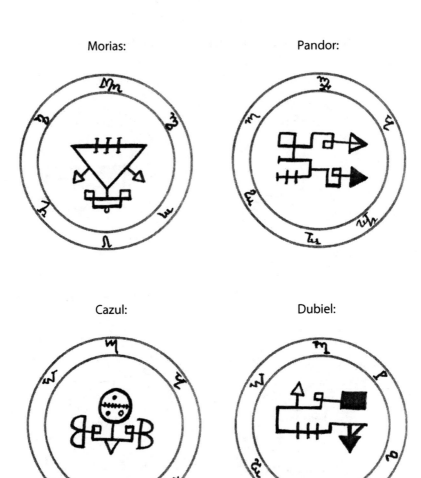

Raysael:

Raysael is a king who rules in the north, he is accompanied by fifty dukes in the day and the same number during the hours of the night. The sixteen spirits that are given that belong to the day are of a good nature and are willing to obey. Whereof the fourteen spirits that are given that belong to the hours of the night are of an evil nature and are not to be trusted for they will not obey willingly. Their seals are to be drawn in green inks.

His traditional conjuration:

'Raysiel afruano chameron fofiel onear vemabi parnothon fruano Caspiel fufre bedarym bulifeor pean curmaby layr vayme pesarym adoreus odiel Vernabi paaeha darsum laspheno devior camedonton phorsy lasbenay to charmon Druson olnays, Venovym lulefon, peorso fabelrotos thurno. Calephoy vem, nabelron bural thorasyn charnoty capelron.'

The sixteen dukes of the day:

Baciar:

Thoac:

Sequiel:

Sadar:

Terath:

Astael:

Ramica:

Dubarus:

Armena:

Albhadur:

Chanaei:

Fursiel:

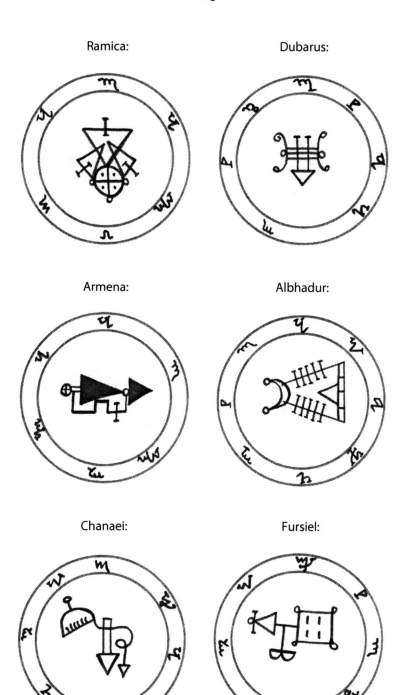

Betasiel:

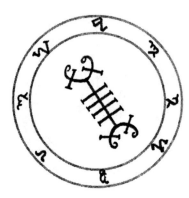

Melcha:

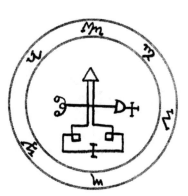

Tharas:

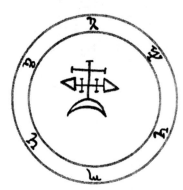

Vriel:

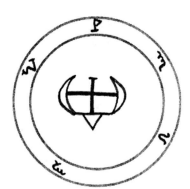

The fourteen dukes that belong to the night:

Thariel: Paras:

Arayl: Culmar:

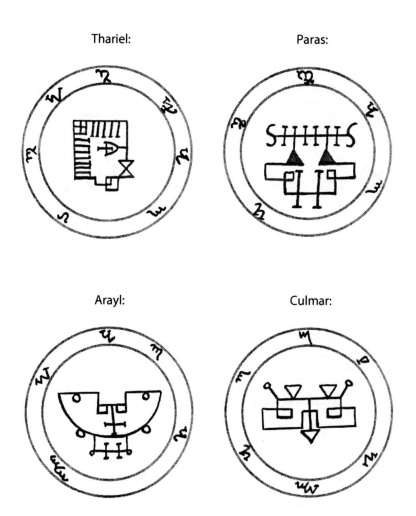

Lazaba:

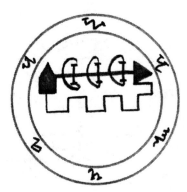

Aleasi:

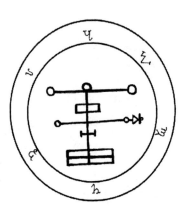

Sebach:

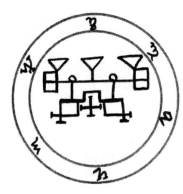

Quibda:

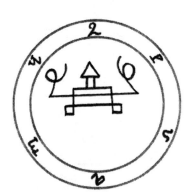

Belsay:

Morael:

Sarach:

Arepach:

Lamas:

Thurcal:

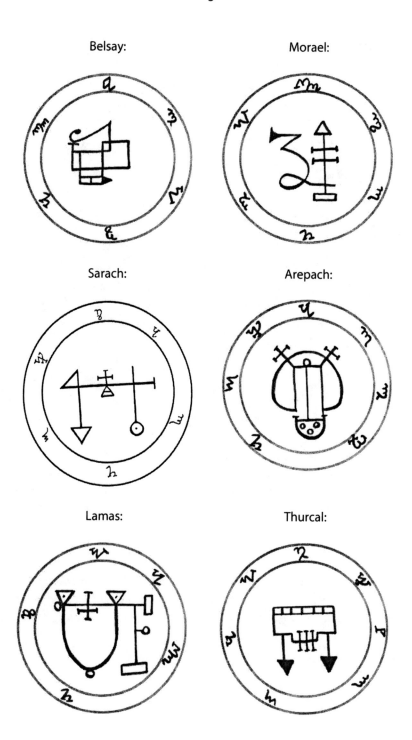

Symiel:

Symiel rules as a king in the north-eastern part of the compass. He has ten dukes that attend by day and ten spirits that are of the night. Their seals are to be drawn in green inks. These spirits do not appear quickly.

His traditional conjuration:

> 'Symiel myrno chamerony theor pasron adiveal fanerosthi sofear Carmedon Charnothiel peasor sositran fabelrusy thyrno pamerosy trelno chabelron chymo churmabon, asiel peasor carmes nabeyros toys Camalthonty.'

The ten spirits of the day:

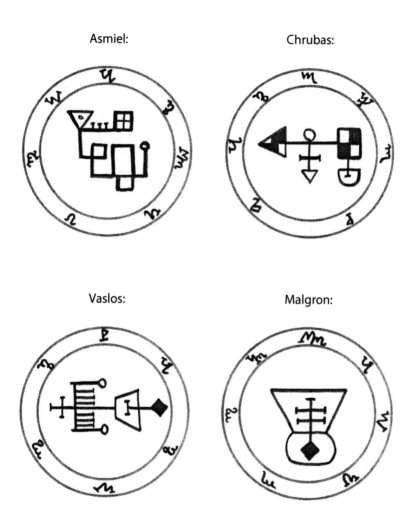

Asmiel:

Chrubas:

Vaslos:

Malgron:

Romiel:

Larael:

Achot:

Bonyel:

Dagiel:

Musor:

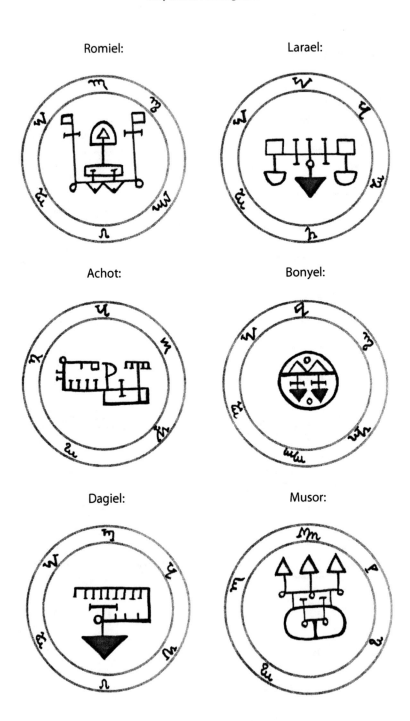

The ten spirits of the night:

Mafrus:

Apiel:

Curiel:

Molael:

Arafos:

Marianu:

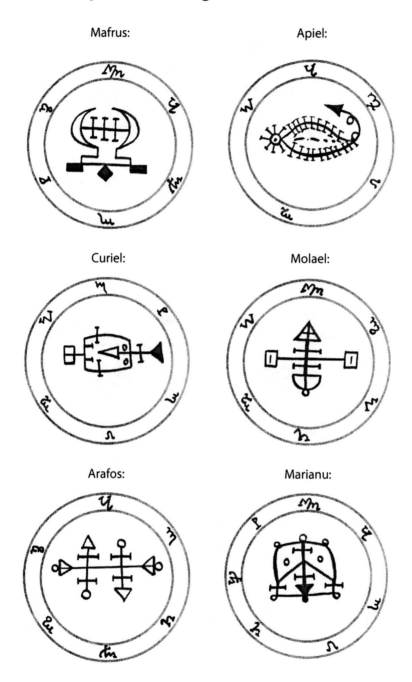

Narzael:

Murahe:

Richel:

Nalael:

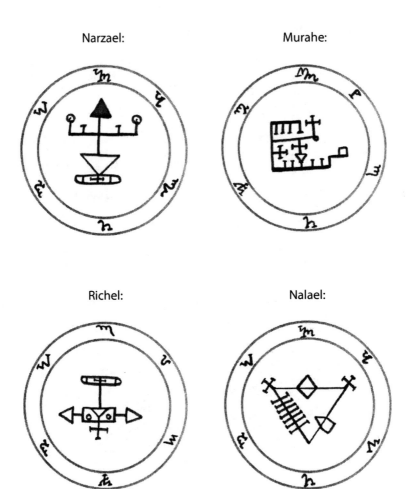

Armadiel:

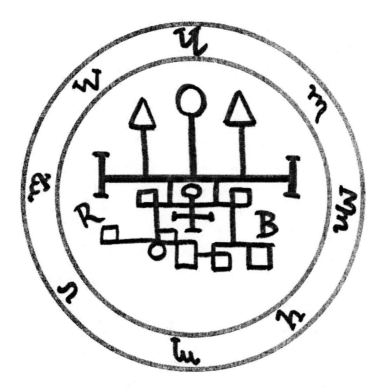

Armadiel is under the Emperor of the North and rules in the north-eastern quarter of the compass. The seals given are for the fifteen more prominent of his servants. To call them follow the order that is given but the day from sunrise to sunset must be divided into fifteen equal parts and these are then allotted to the spirits; the same is done with the hours from sunset to sunrise. Their seals are to be drawn in green inks.

His traditional conjuration:

'Armadiel marbevo pelrusan neor chamyn aldron Pemarson Cathornaor pean lyburmy Caveron thorty abesmeron vear larso charnoty theor Caveos myat drupas Cameldortys ly paruffes ernoty mesoryn elthy chaor atiel, lamesayn rovemu fabelrusin, friato chasalon pheor thamorny mesardiel pelusy madiel baferoty sarreon prolsoyr asenosy camel truson.'

Nassar:

Parabiel:

Lariel:

Calvarnia:

Orariel:

Alferiel:

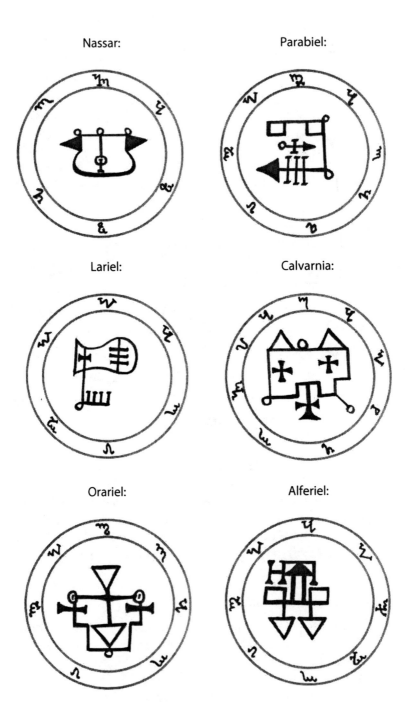

Lariel:

Samiel:

Asmaiel:

Jasziel:

Pandiel:

Carasiba:

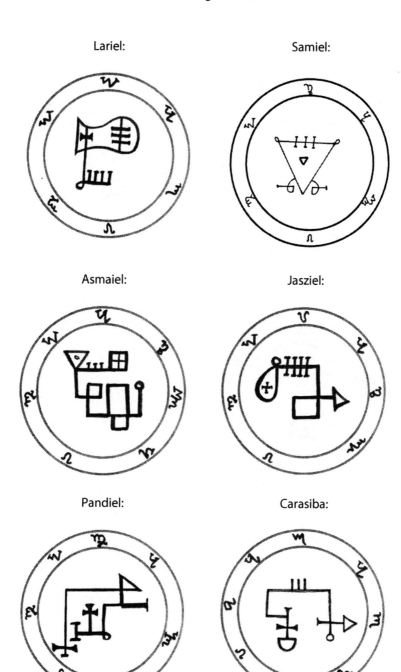

Asbibiel:

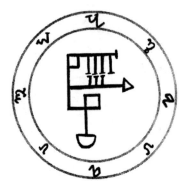

Mafayr:

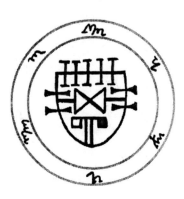

Oemiel

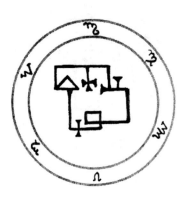

Baruchas:

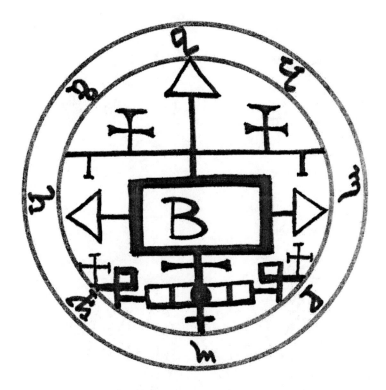

Baruchas is the fourth spirit under the Emperor of the North and rules in the east by north. Of the many spirits under his command fifteen of the chief spirits are given. These spirits are good by nature and are willing to serve the will of the conjuror. To call these spirits the day hours must be divided by fifteen which each period of time allotted to the spirits in the order that they are given. The same with the hours of the night. Their seals are to be drawn green inks.

His traditional conjuration:

'Baruchas malvear chemorsyn charnotiel bason ianocri medusyn aprilty casmyron sayr pean cavoty medason peroel chamyrsyn cherdiel avenos nosear penaon sayr chavelonti genayr pamelron frilcha madyrion onetil fabelronthos.'

Quitta:

Sareal:

Monael:

Cavayr:

Aboc:

Cartael:

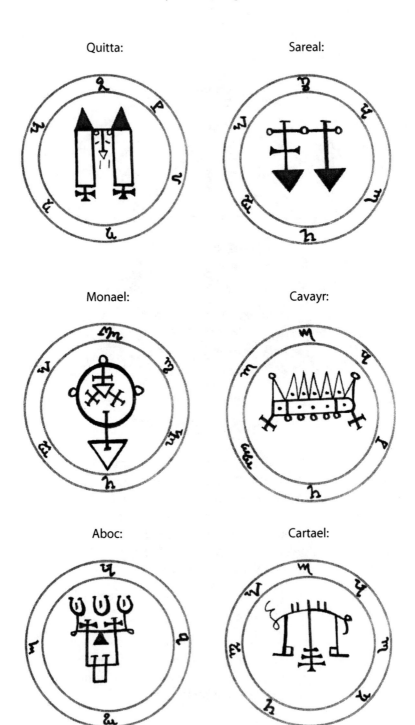

Janiel:

Pharnol:

Baoxas:

Geriel:

Monael:

Chuba:

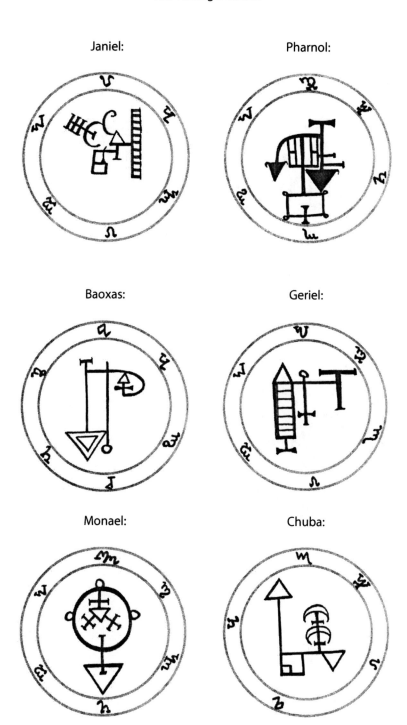

Lamael:

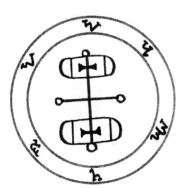

Dorael:

Decaniel:

CHAPTER FOUR

The Wandering Princes

There are fifteen dukes who wander with their retinues in the air. They never stay in one place for long, their natures are both good and evil as I shall indicate accordingly.

The first and chief of these spirits is Geradiel who has many spirits who serve him, but he has no dukes or princes among them. Therefore he is to be conjured alone; however his servants will also appear too. He is to be conjured during the planetary hour of the day, however depending on the hour he will appear with differing numbers of servants. The servants of Geradiel are good by nature and are willing to obey the conjuror in all things.

The seal of Geradiel:

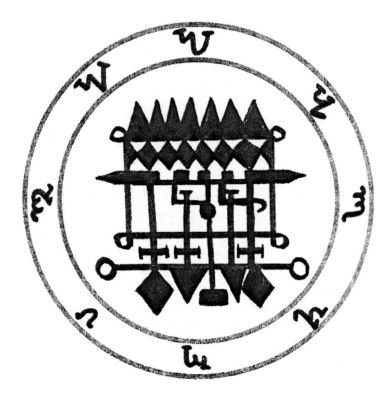

Buriel:

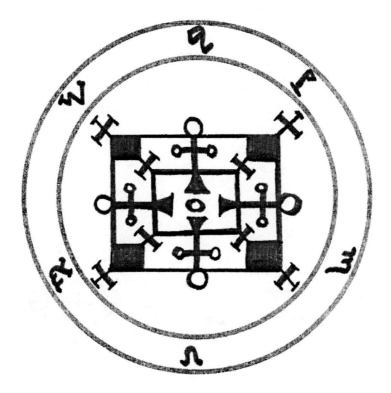

Buriel is the second of the wandering princes and he has many dukes and servants that attend unto him and do his will. They are evil by nature and are hated by the other spirits. The spirits will appear as serpents with the heads of virgins but they will speak with a man's voice. They must be summoned only in the hours of the night for they hate the daylight hours, they must also be summoned during the planetary hour of the night. Each of these dukes has eight hundred and eighty servants that attend unto them. Their seals are to be drawn in green inks. The conjuror must gaze down at the earth when uttering the conjuration and it is better if the conjuration is uttered silently.

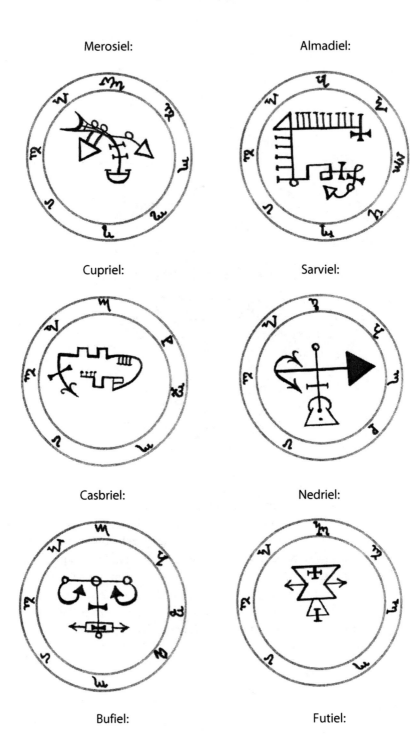

Merosiel:

Almadiel:

Cupriel:

Sarviel:

Casbriel:

Nedriel:

Bufiel:

Futiel:

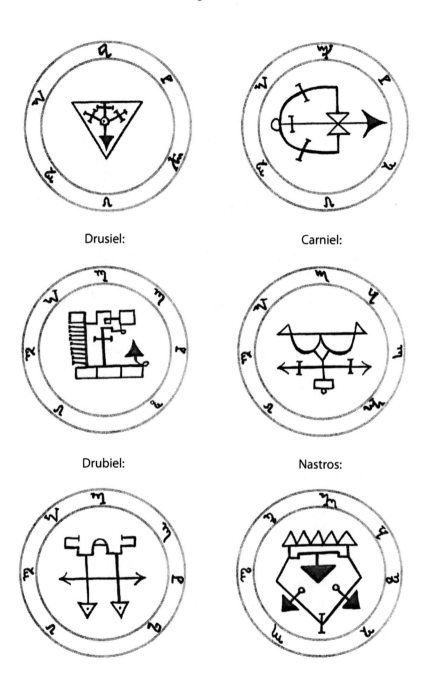

Drusiel:

Carniel:

Drubiel:

Nastros:

Hydriel:

This, the third wandering duke, has three hundred servants who are in attendance and these spirits have servants without number. Given below are the seals of the twelve of the chief dukes. These spirits may be summoned during the day as well as the night time. The first spirit must be summoned during the first of the planetary hours and the second spirit during the second of the planetary hours and so on. These spirits will appear as serpents that have the heads of young girls and are courteous and willing to obey the will of the conjuror. They take pleasure in watery places and this is a good place to summon them. Their seals are to be drawn in green inks.

Mortaliel:

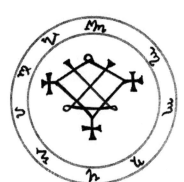

Chamoriel:

Pelariel:

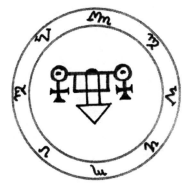

Musuziel:

Lameniel:

Barchiel:

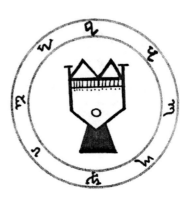

Samiel:

Dusiriel:

Camiel:

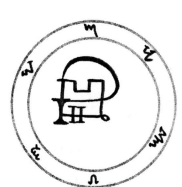

Arbiel:

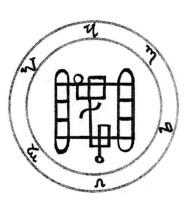

Luciel:

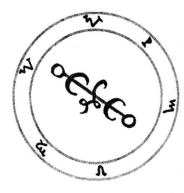

Chariel:

Pirichiel:

The fourth of the wandering dukes is Pirichiel. He is served by eight knights who have two thousand servants who are good by nature and very willing to attend to the conjuror's will. The seals of the spirits are to be drawn in green inks.

Demediel:

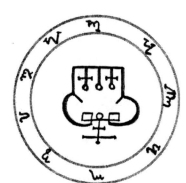

Cardiel:

Almasor:

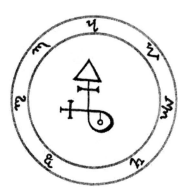

Nemariel:

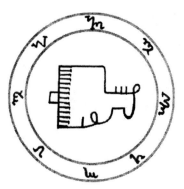

Menariel:

Damarsiel:

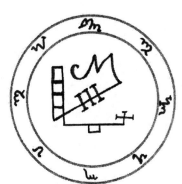

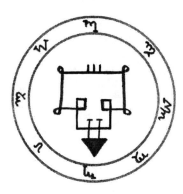

Hursiel:

Cuprisiel:

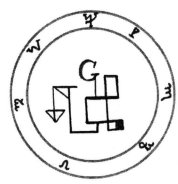

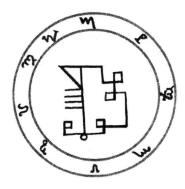

Emoniel:

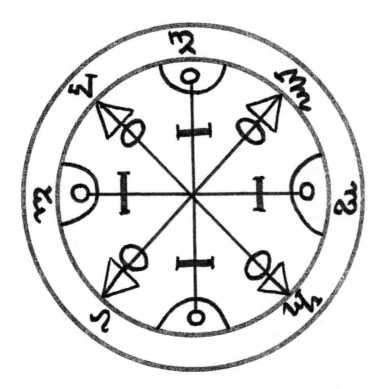

Emoniel is the fifth of the wandering dukes and is served by one hundred spirits. Given below are the seals of twelve of the chief of these spirits who are good by nature and willing to obey the conjuror. They delight in woods and forests and these are best places to summon them; their seals are to be drawn in yellow inks. When summoning any of these spirits they must be summoned in the planetary order of the day with the first spirit being summoned during the first hour of the day and the second spirit during the second hour of the day and so on.

Ermoniel:

Edriel:

Carnodiel:

Phanuel:

Dramiel:

Pandiel:

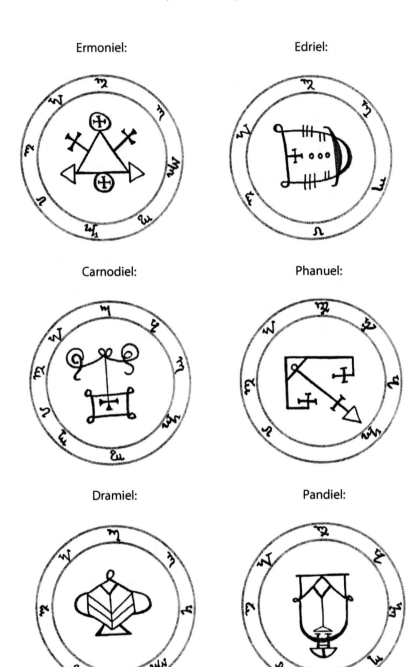

Vasenel:

Nasiniel:

Cruhiel:

Armesiel:

Caspaniel:

Musiniel:

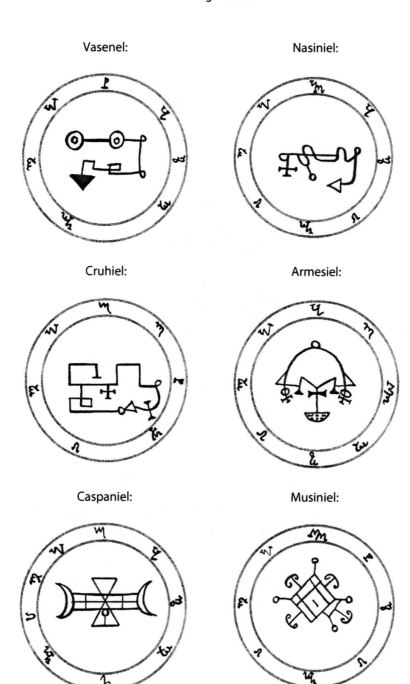

Icosiel:

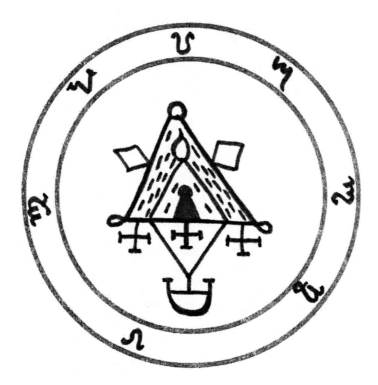

The sixth of the wandering spirits is Icosiel who has four hundred spirits who are in attendance; of whom the seals are given of fifteen of the chief spirits. These spirits are of a good nature and willingly attend to the will of the conjuror. They are easily conjured as they delight in the houses of humans and their company. To summon them the twenty-four hours of the day are to be divided into fifteen with each of the fifteen allotted periods to be given to the spirits in the order that they are given and they are to be summoned therein. The seals of the spirits are to be drawn in yellow inks.

Machariel:

Pischiel:

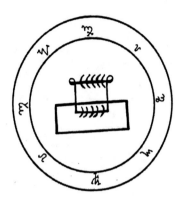

Thanatiel:

Zosiel:

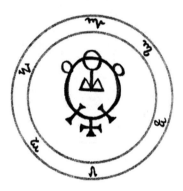

Gapiel:

Larphiel:

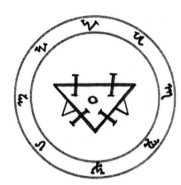

Amediel:

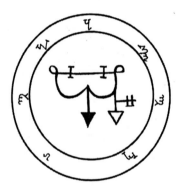

Cambriel:

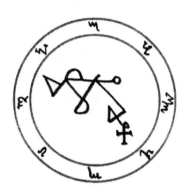

Nathriel:

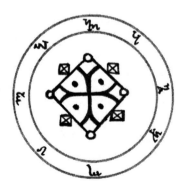

Zachariel:

Athesiel:

Cumariel:

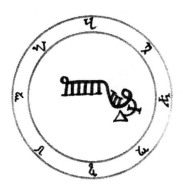

Munefiel:

Heresiel:

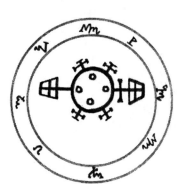

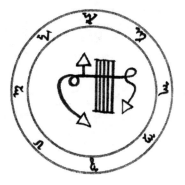

Urbaniel:

Soleviel:

The seventh spirit is Soleviel who has four hundred spirits that are under his command. These spirits are good by nature and are obedient to the will of the conjuror. Given below are the seals of twelve of the more prominent spirits. The spirits are to be allotted to each of the planetary hours in the order that the spirits are given. Their seals are to be drawn in yellow inks.

Inachiel:

Praxeel:

Moracha:

Almodar:

Nadrusiel:

Cobusiel:

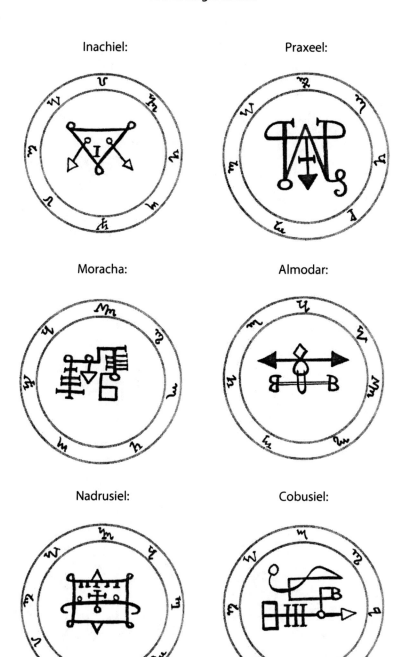

Amriel:

Axosiel:

Charoel:

Prasiel:

Mursiel:

Penador:

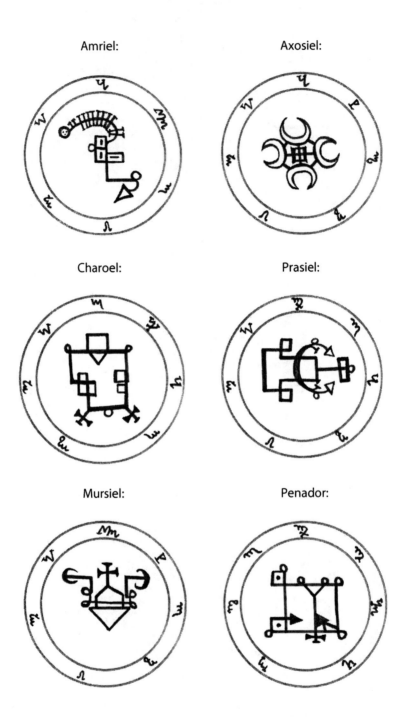

Menadiel:

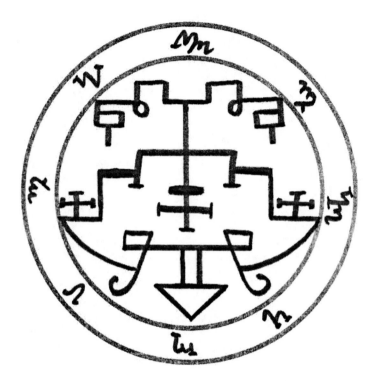

Menadiel is the eighth of the wandering spirits and has twenty dukes and one hundred spirits who are in attendance. These spirits are of a good nature and are obedient to the conjuror, their seals are to be drawn in yellow inks and they are to be summoned in the planetary hour starting with the first spirit in the first hour and the second spirit in the second hour and so forth.

Larmol:

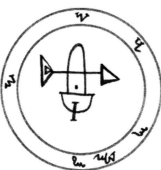

Drasiel:

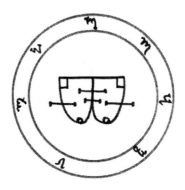

Clamor:

Benodiel:

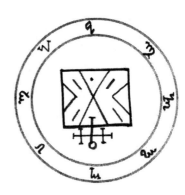

Charisiel:

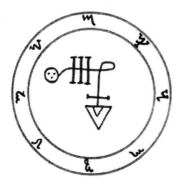

Samyel:

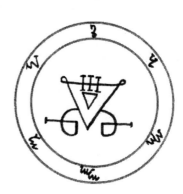

Barchiel:

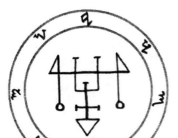

Amasiel:

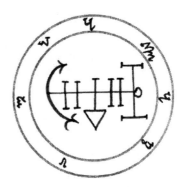

Baruch:

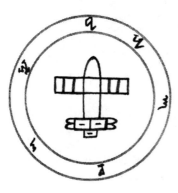

Nedriel:

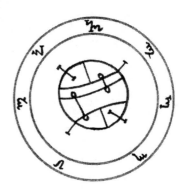

rasin:

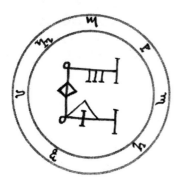

Tharon:

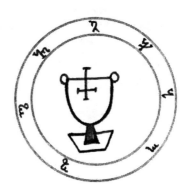

Macariel:

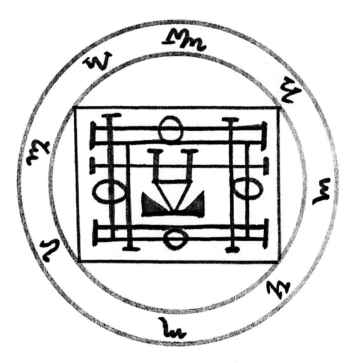

The ninth wandering spirit is Macariel who has forty dukes and many spirits in attendance. These spirits are of a good nature and are willing to obey the conjuror's will in all matters. These spirits may appear in many forms, but they often appear as a dragon with the head of a young girl. They may be called in the hours of the day and the night but they must be summoned during the planetary order of the day starting with the first spirit that is given being allotted to the first hour of the day and so on. Their seals are to be drawn in blue inks.

Claniel:

Drusiel:

Andros:

Charoel:

Asmadiel:

Romyal:

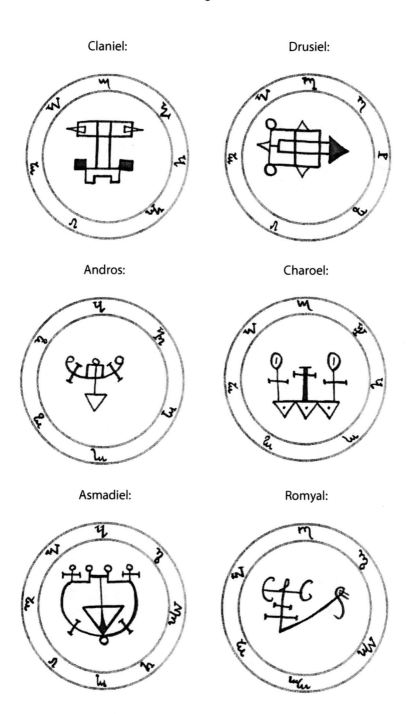

Mastuel:

Varpiel:

Gremiel:

Thuriel:

Brufiel:

Lemodac:

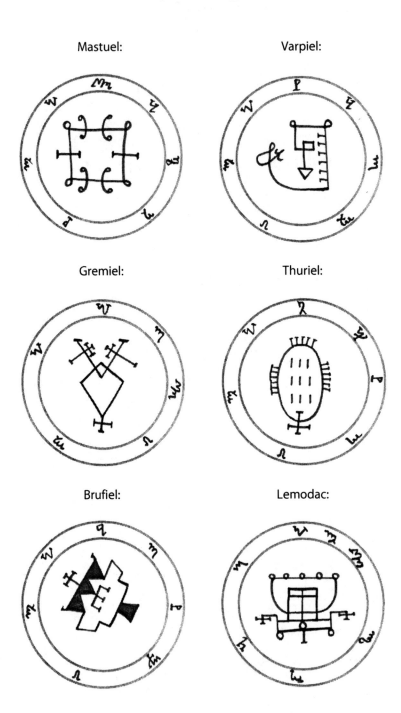

Uriel:

The tenth of the wandering spirits is Uriel who has ten chief spirits and one hundred lesser spirits who are in attendance. These spirits are evil by nature and will not obey the conjuror very readily, nor are they to be trusted. They will appear as serpents that have the head and face of a young girl. Their seals are to be drawn in blue inks.

Chabri:

Drabos:

Narmiel:

Frasmiel:

Brymiel:

Dragon:

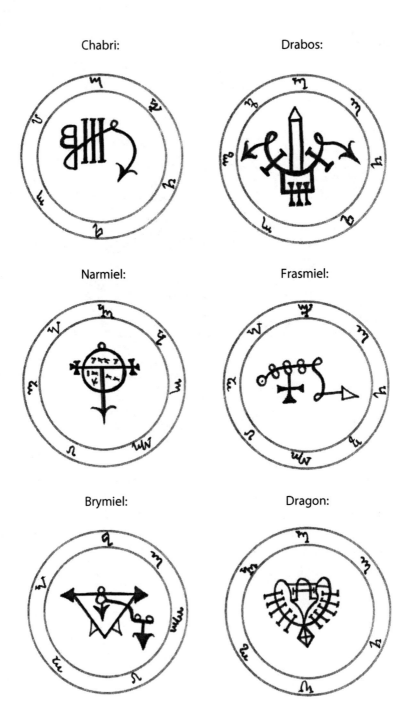

Curmas:

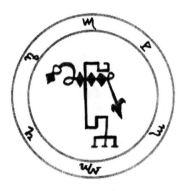

Drapios:

Hermon:

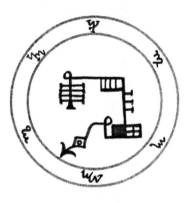

Aldrusy:

Bidiel:

The eleventh and last of the wandering spirits is Bidiel, who is accompanied by twenty dukes and two hundred lesser spirits. These spirits will change their office every year among themselves. All these spirits are good by nature and are willing to obey the conjuror in all matters. They will appear in comely human form and their seals are to be drawn in blue inks.

Mudriel:

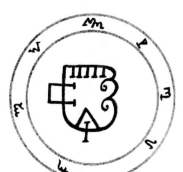

Cruchan:

Bramsiel:

Armoniel:

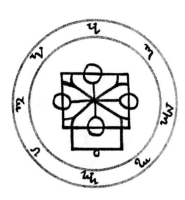

Lameniel:

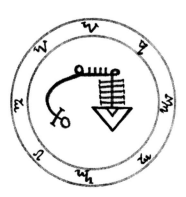

Andruchiel:

Merasiel:

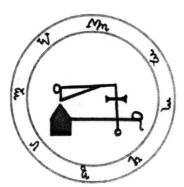

Charobiel:

Parsifiel:

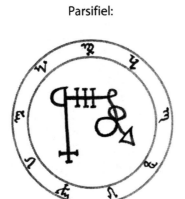

Chremoas:

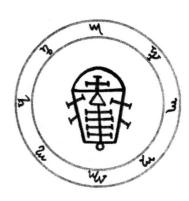

CHAPTER FIVE

Praxis

Firstly I have made the assumption that the reader is familiar with various occult practices from the corpus of the Western Magical Traditions; such as the Lesser Banishing Ritual of the Pentagram (LBRP), the Middle Pillar, and consecrating of the Magical Circle. This also implies that you have the various tools of the arte and are familiar with their use. If not then I recommend *Liber Noctis* as a means to correct this deficiency or perform the following workings for this. The work also calls for hexagram and pentagram lamens; these can be found in the *Goetia* which I have reproduced here. Also I would suggest that you use church incense or frankincense as the suffumigation.

The spirits can be worked with via candle magics, talismans, or by conjuration into the shewstone or indeed visible appearance into the Triangle of Arte, according to your sense of the arte.

Tools of the arte

Of these you will need to have the following tools consecrated and enhallowed; knife with the black hilt, cup, pantacle and wand. You will need a white robe, an aspergillum, the hexagram and pentagram of Solomon, a shewstone and a silken cord for the marking out of the Triangle of Arte, candles and altar cloth, their colours being relevant to the working. An astrological ephemeris will be useful to show which elemental sign the moon is in, as this will deem the best time for the workings. Naturally a suitable working space and an altar are required.

The Knife:

Having found a suitable knife, bury it for three days and nights, thus allowing the earth to absorb its past. Then when the moon is travelling through a fiery sign, (check ephemeris) perform the rite of consecration as thus, although there are other approaches to this working which can be found accordingly.

Being washed and clean, let the altar be draped either in a red cloth with red candles or use white for all the rites that follow:

Perform LBRP.

Consecrate salt and water thus:

Trace over the salt banishing pentagram declaring the following:

> 'Let all malignancy be banished from this salt So that all good may enter therein
> In the name of the God Most High be thou Blessed, dedicated and consecrated to this work.'

Water:

Trace banishing pentagram over the water and say:

> 'I exorcise thee O creature of water that cast out from thee all uncleanliness and deceit. Therefore be thou blessed, dedicated and consecrated to the success of this working
> In the Name of the God Most High.'

Pour salt into water.

Consecration of the fire and incense:

Pointing first and second fingers at the burning charcoal declare:

> 'I exorcise thee O creature of fire that all deceit be banished from thee so that all good may enter here in, in the Names of the God Most High.'

Do the same with the incense before burning it.

Sprinkle water around the edge of the circle saying;

> 'First therefore let the Sorcerer/ess Sprinkle with the lustral waters of the loud resounding sea.'

Take the censer with burning incense around the edge of the circle whilst declaring;

> 'When all the phantasms have vanished thou shall see the holy and formless fire, Hear thou the voice of fire!'

Perform a general invocation such as given or one of your own choosing:

'Blessed art thou Lord of the Universe For thy glory flows out to the ends of creation rejoicing.'

Declare your intention and sprinkle the knife with water and then pass it through the incense smoke. As you do so say the following;

'I conjure thee O knife by the might of the holy names YHVH Tzabaoth and of the Holy Archangel Mikael that thou servest me for a strength and a defence in all operations of the magical arte. Furthermore it is my will that thou attract that which I willest and banish that which I deem so according unto my holy will.'

Trace the invoking pentagram of fire over the altar with the knife and declare that it is now consecrated for the success of all magical acts. Give thanks to the Holy Names of God for the success of the work and close with the LBRP.

Of course rites of consecration can be more complex than the one that I have given, but this will work well for this practice, as at the end of the day it is your intent and will which makes it so, it need only be as complex as your sense of the arte demands. Afterwards wrap the knife in silk cloth.

For the cup, wand and pantacle the following consecrations can be used but the names and colours must be changed accordingly:

Cup:

Direction west. Element water. Colour blue. God Name Elohim Tzabaoth. Archangel Gabriel.

Wand:

Direction east. Element air. Colour yellow. God Name Shaddai El Chai. Archangel Raphael.

Pantacle:

Direction north. Element earth. Colour green. God Name Adonai Ha Aretz. Archangel Auriel.

You will need to write these rites out by hand as this will help to empower them for the workings.

The Lamen, The Ring and The Mirror:

Solomon gives clear designs in the *Goetia* for the lamens, which are required for this work. They can be drawn on parchment or engraved upon a silver disk and worn around the conjuror's neck on a cord or fine chain.

The Pentagram of Solomon:

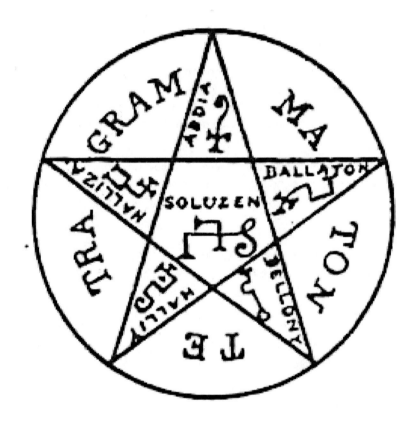

The Hexagram of Solomon:

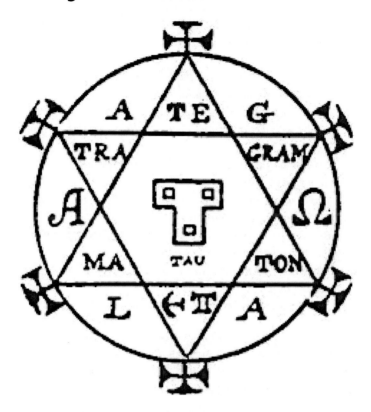

The consecration of the Lamen:

Perform LBRP. Circumbulate with fire and water. State nature of the working. Use suitable invocations for work.

Hold the lamen in the rising smoke of the incense whilst reciting psalm 91.

> 'He who dwells in the shelter of the Most High Who abides in the shadow of the Almighty
> Will say to the Lord, 'My refuge and my fortress, My God in whom I trust.'
> For he will deliver thee from the snare of the fowler And from the deadly pestilence, he will cover thee with his pinions and under his wings thou wilt find refuge, for his faithfulness is a shield and buckler.
> Thou shalt not fear the terror of the night nor the arrow that flies

by day, nor the pestilence that stalks in darkness, nor the destruction that wastes at noonday.
A thousand may fall at thy side ten thousand At thy right side but it will not come near thee. Thou wilt only look with thine eyes and see the recompense of the wicked.
Because thou hath made the Lord thy refuge, the Most High thy habitation, no evil shall befall thee.
No scourge come near thy tent.
For he will give his angels charge of thee to guard thee in all thy ways.
On their hands shalt they bear thee up lest thou shalt dash thy foot against a stone.
Thou wilt tread upon the lion and the adder, the young lion and the serpent wilt thou trample under foot.
Because he cleaves to me in love I will deliver him. I wilt protect him because he knoweth my name.
When he calleth unto me I will answer him I will rescue and honour him.
With long life shall I satisfy him And show him my salvation.'

Now place the lamen around your neck, give thanks for the success of the work and close with LBRP. Use this working for both the Pentagram and Hexagram of Solomon.

The same formula can be used for the consecration of the magical ring of Solomon, which is worn on the middle finger of the left hand. Some speculation has gathered around the shape of the ring as to whether it is a ring in the conventional sense or simply a flat disk with a finger hole in the middle. I suggest that you use a ring of silver with the following names marked on the outer and the inner as given.

Names on the outer – Anepheneton. Mikael. inside the ring – Tetragrammaton.

The Aspergillum:

This is used to sprinkle water around the edge of the circle and is made of the following herbs; vervain, fennel, lavender, sage, valerian, mint, basil, rosemary and hyssop.

Failing this a small bunch of hyssop will suffice. These herbs are bound with a thread that has never been used for anything else. If these are gathered at the full moon and words of blessing said over them they will suffice for the workings.

The Mirror:

The use of mirrors in magic is of great antiquity and a book in itself could be written concerning their use. However, if you are using a shewstone for this it will need a stand to place it upon the altar. The mirror can be consecrated as such at the full moon as it is lunar by nature. Use lunar colours and incense for this rite of consecration.

Perform LBRP. Circumbulate with fire and water. State the intent of the working. Invocations for help with the consecration of the work. Consecrate the stone or mirror with fire and water. Trace invoking hexagram of lunar over the mirror and spend some moments just gazing into the stone. Cover in a silk cloth and close the rite in the usual manner. Afterwards the stone or mirror that you are working with can be placed outside under the full moon to capture its rays. This is a good idea at each full moon but the mirror must be brought inside before sunrise.

It would be wise to have a separate pen and coloured inks for the work, particularly if they have been consecrated to the arte and used solely for magical workings. All that is used in the arte will need to be treated as such and kept separate from the everyday as this helps mark them down as being special, which of course they are.

The Circle and Triangle of Arte:

The circle is more than a defensive creation, whilst it can be seen as such, and indeed with some approaches to conjuration it is such. The circle is a means of limiting your working space so that your concentration is focused upon the area in which you are working - this will add momentum to the working. The triangle will concentrate the energy of the work as the energies will manifest therein, it will also contain the spirit which will make it easier to control it.

With the approach that is outlined here the triangle is marked out upon the top of the altar with a silken cord, it is consecrated with fire and water and with the traditional *Goetia* names that are associated with the triangle of arte.

The triangle must not be broken or crossed until the spirit has been licensed to depart back to its realms. Then and only then can the barrier be crossed when the banishing has taken place. The seal of the spirit will need to be consecrated and placed in the triangle under the shewstone for the duration of the working, with a second seal being fixed on the back of the Pentacle of Solomon which the conjuror is wearing around their neck. Afterwards it must be kept safe and can be used as a talismanic figure which relates to the work that has been performed.

The design for the altar top which is taken from the Seal of Solomon:

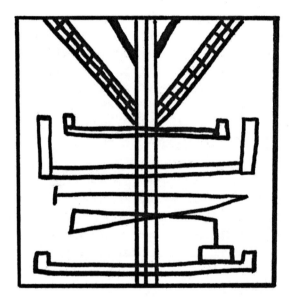

Having decided upon the spirit that you are working with, and whether you intend to work with it by inscribing its name or sigil upon a candle of the relevant colour, and then summoning them, you must state the aim of the work; this must be within their office. At the height of the working, after the conjuring of the spirit, simply light the candle and let it burn out. The spirit must first be decided upon and the triangle must point in the direction from which they will come, that is their compass point, to which will be addressed the conjuration. The Solomonic texts tell us that for this work choose an upstairs room, one that is secret if possible or at least private. If that is not possible use a secluded spot in a wood or somewhere where you will not be disturbed.

Purity of mind and body are of utmost importance. The conjuror must refrain from all irrelevant activity for three days prior to the working. A week would be better still but the demands of life may make this difficult. Daily meditation upon the work in hand will help to concentrate the mind upon the work to come. If you are not a vegetarian then do not eat meat for several days prior to the workings, and for the last twenty-four hours fast, or take a little fruit and bread at the most. Water will be preferable to coffee or tea to drink, therefore do not take alcohol or drugs, medication would be acceptable as it probably could not be avoided.

Washing prior to the conjuration is important, as will be the donning of a clean white robe, preferably one that has been made from pure linen. The washing will need to be done with intent that all negativity is being washed from the mind, body and spirit of the conjuror. Pour a jug of consecrated water over your head whilst reciting the following lines from *Psalm* 51.

> 'Purge me with hyssop O Lord and I shalt be clean.
> Wash me and I shalt be whiter than snow.'

When putting on the white robe say;

> 'By the figurative mystery of these holy vestures I will clothe me with the armour of salvation
> In the strength of the highest.
> Ancor Amacor Amides Theodonias Anitor that my desired end maybe effected through ye strength of Adonai to whom all praise and glory will for ever belong.
> Amen.'

Let there now be prayers and invocations to God for the success of the work to come.

The four Great Emperors at the compass points are

Carnesiel – east, Caspiel – south, Ameradiel –west, Demoriel – north

The conjurations:

> 'For I XYZ conjure thee O spirit ABC
> Thou who art the Emperor of (state compass point) That thou by the Holy Names of God Most High, and unto whom all things obey that thou manifest here within this shewstone speaking words of truth and understanding.

*Furthermore that thou dost return unto thy realms when thou art
licensed to do so without causing any harm or fear to anyone or
anything.*

*For I XYZ, made in the image of God loved by God and imbued
with his holy power do so by the might of his Holy Names do
conjure thee that thou art obedient unto this my holy will!'*

Also of use are the conjurations that are given for each of the
spirits; these are from the *Steganographia* and can be used after the
general invocation of the spirit. You may have to repeat the
conjurations several times. If you feel that there is no physical
manifestation that does not mean that the spirit is not present.
Therefore declare your will and do not forget or ignore the License to
Depart. This conjuration can be adapted if you are using candle magic
to work with the spirit by changing the wording accordingly.

If you are endeavouring to work with the spirit via candle magics
then you will not need a manifestation of the spirit concerned. Just a
general clear and concise statement of the work in hand will be
sufficient for your purpose.

The Conjuration of the Wandering Princes:

*'For I XYZ, do conjure thee O spirit ABC, who wandereth here and
there in the air with thy dukes and others of thy servants.*

*For I conjure thee that thou doest forthwith come and appear in
this holy shewstone of the arte that is here before me.*

*Come thou in comely form speaking words of truth and
understanding unto me.*

*Be thou attentive unto my will for I who art a servant of the God
Most High do command thee by his Holy Names that thou art
appear now within this shewstone of the arte as I do will.'*

Use also the *Steganographia* conjurations as given. Repeat the
conjurations again if necessary and also adapt them; if working with the
spirit via candle magics as previously stated.

The conjuration of the spirits:

*'For I XYZ, do conjure thee
O thou Mighty and Potent spirit ABC who ruleth under the Prince
or King N in the dominion of (state direction)
For I conjure thee O spirit N that thou come forth and appeareth*

within this shewstone of the arte here before me. Come thou in comely form and be thou attentive unto my will in all matters.

For I conjure and powerfully command thee O spirit N by him who said the word and it was done and by all the holy and powerful names of God and by the name of the One Creator of Heaven, Earth and Hell and that which is contained therein.

Adony, El, Elohim, Elohe, Elion, Escerchie, Zebaoth Jah, Tetragrammaton, Saday.

The Lord God of the Hosts that you forthwith appear unto me here in this shewstone in comely form without causing harm nor fear to myself or any living creature.

Come thou peaceably, affably and visibly now without delay manifesting what I desire, being conjured by the name of the eternal living and true God:

Helioren Tetragrammaton, Anephexeton and fulfill my commands and persist therein unto the end.

For I conjure command and constrain thee O spirit N. by Alpha Omega.

By the name Primeumaton, which commandeth the whole host of heaven and by all those names which Moses named when he by the power of those names brought great plagues upon Pharoah and all the people of Egypt.

Zebaoth, Escerchie, Oriston, Elion, Adonay, Primeumaton, and by the name Schemes Amathia with which Joshua called upon and the sun stayed his course and by the name of Hagios and by the seal of Adonay and by Agla, On, Tetragrammaton.

To whom all creatures are obedient and by the dreadful judgment of the High God and by the Holy Angels of heaven
and by the mighty wisdom of the Great God of Hosts.

That you come from all parts of the world and make rational answers unto all things I shall ask of thee.

And come you peaceably, visibly and affably speaking unto me with a voice intelligent and to my understanding.

Therefore come, come ye in the name of Adonay, Zebaoth, Adony, Amioram.

Come, why stay thee, hasten Adonay Saday the King of Kings commandeth thee!'

Again adapt if using with candle magic as no manifestation will be required with this working.

The Arte of Conjuration:

Conjuration is probably the most spectacular of the occult artes and it is certainly demanding. One will need a good understanding of occult praxis and theories for this type of working and is therefore more suited to those who have some experience of such artes. However the spirits can be accessed by candle magics as they can by other forms of the arte which will allow the early student to feel that they are not out of their depth with this aspect of the arte, which no doubt they will find useful. Spirits do not always appear as such and are easier to work with via the magic mirror or shewstone than working for a full conjuration to visible appearance which isn't necessary for the magic to work. Regardless of psychological theories concerning the nature of spirits and whether they are simply manifestations of one's complexes etc; which has become a point of view in some quarters, you will be advised to respect the spirits, on their own terms and not as an aspect of one's own psyche which can be bossed about.

On the whole, the spirits of the *Theugia Goetia* seem to be quite a versatile lot, whereas spirits generally have distinct offices to fulfill, some spirits being easier to work with then others.

Modus:

Having gathered the requirements and having drawn the seals in their elemental colours, let the conjuror be washed and robed according to the demands of our arte. Therefore in a suitable place let the circle be drawn as given below.

The Circle:

East

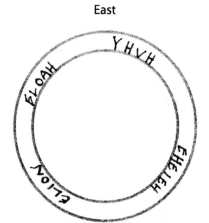

The altar is to be laid out thus:

East

Candle   Oil of Abra-Melin   Candle

Wand

Pantacle with Salt   Black-handled Knife

Triangle

Equal sided marked with silken cord

Place shewstone therein with consecrated seal

Book of Arte   Censer

Sword

Give prayers to God for the success of the working and mark your brow with the holy oil of Abra-Melin. This being a sign of the link between your lower self and your higher self, thus placing the workings under the auspices of the higher aspects of your being.

Continue with the Kabbalistic Cross and Lesser Banishing Ritual of the Pentagram (LBRP), the consecration of the salt and water, dedication of candles, incense and the fire (burning charcoal). The triangle must be marked out with the seal inside and the shewstone placed over the seal.

Bless the boundaries of the triangle with the holy water and cense the boundaries of the triangle with the perfumes of the arte too. This is done with the firm conviction that nothing will cross over the boundaries. Then trace over the three sides of the triangle with the knife or sword, whilst seeing the triangle glowing with a bright light. Conjure the triangle that nothing will cross the boundaries that you are declaring. Do this in the holy names of Tetragrammaton, Primeumateon, Anaphaxeton and by the names of the holy Archangel Mikael. There are several methods of creating the magical circle; as these spirits are related to the compass points I would suggest that the conjuror uses the pentagrams that are associated with the elements of the compass points. Therefore after the LBRP and the consecrations with fire and water perform this working again but use the invoking pentagrams that are relevant to the working and close with the LBRP.

Face east and declare:

'Holy art thou Lord of the Universe etc'

Then intone:

'I invoke thee ye angels of the Celestial Spheres whose dwelling is in the invisible.
For thou art the Guardians of the Universe be thou guardians of this my sacred sphere. Keep far from me the evil and the unbalanced
Strengthen and inspire me so that I may preserve unsullied this abode of the mysteries of God.
Let my sphere be pure and holy that I may enter therein and become a partaker of the secrets of the light divine.'

Contemplate the sacredness of your space for a few moments, and then proceed with your working. Perform the Middle Pillar working as this will help to connect with your higher self. Then use the relevant conjurations that are given for the spirit that you are working with. It will also help to concentrate the working by tracing with the wand, over the triangle, but without crossing it, the pentagram that is associated with the element of the compass point where the spirit is coming from. Also the conjuration of the spirit must be addressed to the quarter from whence it will come.

When it has manifested or you feel that it is present it must be shown the Hexagram of Solomon.

Saying:

> 'Behold the pentacle of Solomon which I have brought here before thy presence:
> Behold the person of the exorcist in the midst of the exorcism, who armed by God and without fear who potently invoke thee and called you to appear.
> Therefore make rational answers to my demands and be obedient to me your master in the name of Lord Bathat rushing upon Abrac Abeor coming upon Aberer!'

The spirit will now be obedient unto the conjuror who must further test the spirit by the names of God to declare its nature. It will go if it is not the spirit in question that you are endeavouring to work with.

License to Depart:

Under no circumstances are you to omit this part of the working even if you feel that it has been a failure.

> 'O Thou spirit N. thou who hast answered my demands and was ready and willing to come at my call I do hereby License thee to Depart unto thy proper place without doing any injury or danger to any man or beast, depart I say and be ever ready to come at my call, being duly exorcised and conjured by ye sacred rites of magic. For I charge thee to withdraw peaceably and quietly and the peace of God be ever continued between thee and me. Amen.'

Give thanks to God for the success of the working and close with a further circumbulation of the circle with fire and water and a firm LBRP.

Adonai Ached The Lord is One

Further Reading

Ars Salomonis - G. St. M. Nottingham (2015), Avalonia, London

Liber Noctis - G. St. M. Nottingham (2015), Avalonia, London

Practical Candle Magic - M. A. Howard (2005), Ignotus Press

Practical Planetary Magick – D. Rankine & S. d'Este (2007), Avalonia, London

The Goetia of Dr Rudd – S. Skinner & D. Rankine (2007), Golden Hoard Press, Singapore

The Lesser Key of Solomon – J, Peterson (2001), Weiser Books, Maine

The Tree of Life – I. Regardie (2001), Llewellyn, Minnesota

Index

A

Abael 83
Abariel 85
Aboc 114
Abriel 76
Abrulges 30
Achot 106
Acreba 45
Acteras 44
Adan 89
Agapiel 134
Aglas 51
Agor 65
Agra 50
Agrippa, Cornelius 11
Albhadur 99
Aldrusy 147
Aleasi 102
Alferiel 110
Aliel 60, 79
Almadiel 120
Almasor 127
Almesiel 24
Almodar 137
Almoel 91
Althor 74
Amandiel 87
Amasiel 141
Ambri 19
Amediel 134
Amenadiel, Emperor 22, 23
Amenta 85

Amiel 55, 70
Amoyr 62
Amriel 138
Anael 50
Anaphaxeton 164
Andros 143
Andruchiel 149
Anepheneton 156
Aniel 39, 94
Anoyr 29
Ansoel 88
Apiel 107
Arach 61
Arafos 107
Aratiel 39
Arayl 101
Arbiel 125
Arcisat 54
Arean 40
Arepach 103
Aresiel 16
Aridiel 20
Ariel 54
Arios 67
Armadiel 109
Armany 15
Armena 99
Armesiel 131
Armoniel 149
Arnen 85
Arnibiel 26
Aroan 51

Aroc 68
Aroziel 80
Artino 72
Asahel 40
Asbibiel 112
Aseliel 38
Asimiel 36
Asmadiel 143
Asmaiel 111
Asmiel 105
Asoriel 94
Aspar 70
aspergillum 151, 156
Asphiel 40
Asphor 75
Aspiel 56, 69
Assaba 48
Assuel 60
Astael 98
Astib 46
Astor 53
Asuriel 91
Asyriel 52
Athesiel 135
Atniel 59
Atriel 63
Auriel, Archangel 153
Axosiel 138
Azemo 37
Azimel 59

B

Baabal 46
Bachiel 62
Baciar 98
Balsur 24
Baoxas 115
Barbil 44
Barbis 45
Barchiel 124, 141
Barfas 67

Barfos 89
Bariel 49
Barmiel 42
Baros 62
Barsu 87
Baruch 141
Baruchas 113
Basiel 70
Belsay 103
Benodiel 140
Benoham 15
Betasiel 100
Bidiel, Wandering Prince 148
Bofar 41
Bonyel 106
Borasy 65
Bramsiel 149
Brufiel 144
Brymiel 146
Budar 56
Budarim 19
Budiel 34
Bufiel 120
Bulis 78
Buniel 53
Burfa 89
Buriel, Wandering Prince 119
Burisiel 26
Busiel 77

C

Cabariel 92
Cabarim 26
Cabrel 66
Cabron 22, 76
Cadriel 83
Calim 36
Calvarnia 110
Cambriel 134
Camiel 22, 23, 125
Camor 21

Camory 21
Camuel........................... 33
Camyel........................... 34
Caniel 45
Capriel..................... 16, 17
Carasiba........................111
Carba 73
Cardiel..........................127
Carga 53
Cariel............................ 35
Carmiel.......................... 65
Carnesiel, Emperor 14, 15, 29, 159
Carniel..........................121
Carnodiel.......................130
Carnol 27
Caron 69
Carpiel........................... 44
Carsiel........................... 73
Cartael..........................114
Casael 77
Casbriel.........................120
Casiel 66
Caspaniel.......................131
Caspiel, Emperor . 18, 19, 42, 97, 159
Cavayr 114
Cayros 82
Cazul............................. 96
Chabri...........................146
Chamiel 27
Chamoriel 123
Chamos.......................... 41
Chanaei.......................... 99
Chansi 43
Charas 39
Chariel.....................20, 125
Charisiel........................140
Charobiel.......................150
Charoel 138, 143
Chasor 59

Chremoas.......................150
Chrubas 105
Chuba...........................115
Churibal 27
Cirecas........................... 51
Citgara 34
Clamor 140
Claniel 143
Clyssan 94
Cobusiel 137
Codriel 24
Coliel............................ 48
Cruchan 149
Cruhiel 131
Cubi 68
Cubiel 39
Cugiel 95
Culmar 101
Cumariel........................135
Cumeriel 17
cup 151, 153
Cuphal........................... 94
Cupriel 120
Cuprisiel 128
Curasin..........................141
Curiel 40, 107
Curifas 24
Curmas..........................147
Cursas........................... 79
Cusiel 54
Cusriel 55
Cusyne 80

D

Dabrinos......................... 27
Dagiel...........................106
Damarsiel.......................127
Danael........................... 76
Daniel 35
Darbori.......................... 79
Decaniel 116

Deilas.................................. 70
Demediel............................128
Demoriel, Emperor ...25, 26, 159
Diviel.................................. 76
Dobiel.................................. 36
Dodiel.................................. 68
Dorael................................116
Doriel.................................. 26
Dorochiel 71
Dorothiel...............See Dorochiel
Drabos................................146
Dragon................................146
Dramiel..............................130
Drapios 147
Drasiel................................140
Drubiel................................121
Drusiel........................... 121, 143
Dubarus..............................99
Dubiel..................................96
Dubilon................................27
Dusiriel..............................124

E

Earos.................................. 63
Earviel................................ 58
Ebra.................................... 30
Edriel.................................130
Efiel 72, 74
Elcar................................... 34
Eliel.................................... 62
Elitel................................... 94
Emoniel, Wandering Prince.129
Emuel 75
Ermoniel............................130
Espoel................................ 60
Ethiel.................................. 91
Etimiel 94

F

Fabariel.............................. 88
Fabiel................................. 73
Faseau................................ 56

Femol 21
Frasmiel.............................146
Fursiel................................ 99
Futiel............................82, 120

G

Gabio.................................. 46
Gabriel, Archangel.................153
Gariel................................. 81
Garnasu 87
Gediel................................. 47
Geradiel, Wandering Prince117, 118
Geriel...........................19, 115
Godiel........................... 88, 93
Goetia 11, 12, 151, 154, 157, 166
Gremiel...............................144
Gudiel................................. 75

H

Hamas 56
Hamorphiel 31
Heresiel..............................135
Hermon 147
Hexagram of Solomon 155, 156, 165
Hissam 87
Hursiel...............................128
Hydriel, Wandering Prince...122

I

Icosiel, Wandering Prince.....132
Inachiel..............................137
Itrasbiel.............................. 31
Itules................................. 31

J

Janiel.................................115
Jasziel................................111

K

Kabbalistic Cross 164

Keriel 43
knife 151, 153, 164

L

Ladiel 95
Lamael 23, 116
Lamas 103
lamen 12, 155, 156
Lameniel 124, 149
Laphor 16
Larael 106
Larfos 77
Lariel 110
Larmol 21, 140
Larphiel 134
Las Pharon 91
Lazaba 102
LBRP 151, 152, 153, 155, 156,
   157, 164, 165, See Lesser
   Banishing Ritual of the
   Pentagram
Lemodac 144
Lesser Banishing Ritual of the
   Pentagram 151
Liber Noctis 151, 166
Libiel 68
Lodiel 83
Lomor 77
Luciel 125
Luziel 23

M

Macariel, Wandering Prince . 142
Machariel 133
Mador 26, 95
Madriel 29
Mafayr 112
Mafrus 107
Magael 72
Magni 86
Mahue 58
Malgaras 64

Malgron 105
Malguel 54
Maniel 72
Mansi 44
Marae 90
Maras 20, 61
Mareaiza 46
Marguns 45
Marianu 107
Mariel 39
Maroth 55
Maseriel 57
Mashel 49
Mastuel 144
Maziel 81
Medar 27
Melas 41
Melcha 100
Melchon 114
Meliel 65
Menadiel, Wandering Prince
   139
Menador 26
Menariel 128
Merach 74
Meras 36
Merasiel 150
Merosiel 120
Meroth 83
Middle Pillar 151, 164
Mikael, Archangel 156, 164
mirror 157, 162
Misiel 67
Molael 107
Momel 78
Monael 115
Moracha 137
Morael 103
Morias 96
Moriel 37
Mortaliel 123

Moziel.................................82
Mudriel 149
Munefiel 135
Murahe 108
Mursiel 138
Musiniel 131
Musiriel 23
Musor 106
Musuziel 123
Myresyn 15

N

Nadrel 31
Nadroc 22, 24
Nadrusiel 137
Nahiel 78
Nalael 108
Naras.................................48
Narmiel 146
Narsiel 82
Narzael 108
Nasiniel 131
Nassar..............................110
Nastros.............................121
Nathriel 134
Nedriel 120, 141
Nemariel...........................127
Neriel 35
Nodar 36
Noguiel 61

O

Odiel 41
Ofisiel 78
Omiel...........................55, 74
Omyel................................34
Orariel 110
Oriel 20, 67
Ormenu 30
Ornich 15
Orpemiel 34
Oryn.................................111

Ossiediel............................90
Othiel.................................41
Otim...................................95

P

Padiel................................32
Pafiel.................................81
Pamersiel 28, 29
Pandiel......................111, 130
Pandor 96
Paniel.................................79
pantacle 151, 153
Parabiel............................110
Paracelsus..........................11
Paras................................101
Pariel.................................35
Parius................................93
Parniel...............................39
Parsifiel.............................150
Pathier................................90
Patiel.................................60
Pelariel.............................123
Pelusar...............................80
Penador.............................138
Peniel.................................95
Pentacle of Solomon.............158
Pentagram of Solomon154, 156
Phaniel...............................36
Phanuel 130
Pharnol.............................115
Pirichiel, Wandering Prince..126
Pischiel.............................133
Potiel 86
Prasiel...............................138
Praxeel 137
Primeumateon.....................164

Q

Quibda..............................102
Quitta...............................114

R

Rabas 53
Rabiel 63, 66
Rablion 31
Raboc 69
Ramica 99
Ranciel 49
Raphael, Archangel 153
Rapsiel 23
Raysael 97
Reciel 50
Richel 108
Romiel 106
Romyal 143
Roriel 58

S

Sabas 48
Sadar 98
Saddiel 89
Sadiel 50
Saemiel 61
Safern 86
Salvor 63
Samiel 111, 124
Samyel 140
Sarach 103
Sareal 114
Sariel 41, 49
Sarviel 120
Satifiel 93
Seal of Solomon 158
Sebach 102
Sequiel 98
shewstone 11, 12, 151, 157, 158,
   159, 160, 161, 162, 163, 164
Sochas 43
Sodiel 90
Soleviel, Wandering Prince ..136
Soriel 75, 81
Sotheano 30

Steganographia 11, 12, 15, 18,
   160
Suriel 73
Symiel 104

T

Taros 93
Tediel 37
Terath 98
Tetragrammaton .. 156, 161, 164
Thalbus 95
Thanatiel 133
Tharas 100
Thariel 101
Tharon 141
Theurgia Goetia 11, 162
Thoac 98
Thurcal 103
Thuriel 144
Tigara 43
Triangle of Arte 151, 157, 158,
   164, 165
Trithemius 11, 18
Tugaros 37

U

Udiel 66
Urbaniel 135
Uriel, Wandering Prince 145
Ursiel 19
Usiel 84
Usiniel 88

V

Vadriel 17
Vadros 22, 23
Varpiel 144
Vasenel 131
Vaslos 105
Vessur 59
Vraniel 80
Vriel 51, 100

Index

W

wand........................ 151, 153, 165

Z

Zabriel... 16

Zachariel 134
Zamor...69
Zeriel 58
Zoeniel...24
Zosiel...133

FOUNDATIONS OF PRACTICAL SORCERY

A seven-volume set of magical treatises, unabridged, comprising:

Vol. I - Liber Noctis

A Handbook of the Sorcerous Arte

Liber Noctis explores the attitudes, training and preparation required for success in ritual, and, as the title suggests, does not shy away from the 'darker' aspects of magic. Practical, experiential, lucid and non-judgmental, this book lays the groundwork for the successful study and practice of sorcery in the modern world.

Vol. II - Ars Salomonis

Being of that Hidden Arte of Solomon the King

Ars Salomonis is a practical manual for working with the talismanic figures found in the Key of Solomon, the most significant of all grimoires. Including two methods for empowering and activating the planetary pentacles, the author makes this vital work safely accessible to beginners. It is an ideal entranceway into the grimoire tradition.

Vol. III - Ars Geomantica

Being an account and rendition of the Arte of Geomantic Divination and Magic

Ars Geomantica explores the medieval system of Geomancy, one of the simplest and most practical of the divinatory arts. The inclusion of detailed instructions on the creation of geomantic staves, elemental fluid condensers, and talismanic construction and consecration make this work a superb introduction to an extensive assortment of magical and divinatory principles.

Vol. IV - Ars Theurgia Goetia

Being an account and rendition of the Arte and Praxis of the Conjuration of some of the Spirits of Solomon

Ars Theurgia Goetia presents a precise and practical guide to working with the spirits of this neglected text from the Solomonic grimoire cycle, the Theurgia-Goetia, giving the full seals of the spirits for the first time. The complete ritual sequence of preparation, conjuration, and license to depart is lucidly demonstrated, making this work suitable for both the beginner and the experienced practitioner.

Vol. V - Otz Chim

The Tree of Life

Otz Chim is a practical exploration of the magic of the Kabbalistic Tree of Life, the glyph that concentrates the essence of magic and mysticism within the Western Mystery Tradition. This book focuses on lesser-known aspects such as the angels associated with the paths, their seals, and invocations and includes the previously unavailable Massa Aborum Vitae.

Vol. VI - Ars Speculum

Being an Instruction on the Arte of using Mirrors and Shewstones in Magic

Ars Speculum is a concise and practical work on the use of mirrors and shewstones in magic. In it the author explores skrying and working with the four elements of air, fire, water and earth - both with elemental condensers and different elemental creatures. Other techniques include contacting other levels of being, the conjuration of spirits, binding and ligature, and healing and protection.

Vol. VII - Liber Terriblis

Being an Instruction on the seventy-two Spirits of the Goetia

Liber Terribilis is a practical study of how to work with the seventy-two spirits of the infamous seventeenth-century Grimoire, the Goetia. It also explores the vital and often neglected use of the seventy-two binding angels of the Great Name of God, the Schemhamphorasch. This volume will be of value to all levels of students and practitioners of the grimoire traditions, being based upon the work of a small group of occultists who have explored it in practice.

More information available on the Avalonia website-
www.avaloniabooks.co.uk

Or write to:
BM Avalonia
London
WC1N 3XX
England, United Kingdom

Readers who found Foundations of Practical Sorcery of interest, is likely to enjoy:

A Collection of Magical Secrets & a Treatise of mixed Cabalah by Stephen Skinner and David Rankine

Climbing the Tree of Life by David Rankine

Living Theurgy by Jeffrey S. Kupperman

Practical Elemental Magick by Sorita d'Este and David Rankine

The Book of Gold by David Rankine & Paul Harry Barron (trans.)

The Book of Treasure Spirits, edited by David Rankine

The Complete Grimoire of Pope Honorius by David Rankine & Paul Harry Barron (trans.)

The Cunning Man's Handbook by Jim Baker

The Grimoire of Arthur Gauntlet by David Rankine

Thoth by Lesley Jackson

Thracian Magic by Georgi Mishev

Wicca Magickal Beginnings by Sorita d'Este and David Rankine

CPSIA information can be obtained
at www.ICGtesting.com
Printed in the USA
LVOW08s0807010617

536565LV00002B/322/P